The Ranch Papers

The Ranch Papers

A California Memoir

JANE HOLLISTER WHEELWRIGHT

The Lapis Press
SANTA MONICA · SAN FRANCISCO

Copyright © Jane Hollister Wheelwright 1988
All rights reserved
Published in 1988 by The Lapis Press
1850 Union Street #466
San Francisco, Calif. 94123

Second Printing, 1988

Library of Congress Cataloging in Publication Data
Wheelwright, Jane Hollister 1905–
The ranch papers
  1. Hollister Ranch (Calif.)
  2. Wheelwright, Jane Hollister–Diaries.
  3. Pipe lines–California.
F869.H73W48   1987   979.4'75   87-80275
ISBN 0-932499-19-8

To Joe, Lynda, and John, with love

Contents

The Ranch Papers

Introduction

WHEN I WAS A CHILD I lived in a world of miracles: the Hollister Ranch, which had belonged to my family for generations but which, in dreams and in memory, became the central part of me. No one would have staked a claim quite like mine nor would they have realized much profit from it if they had; the inventory would have been a hard thing to pin down. When I grew up I moved away to live another kind of life, a city one. I thought that was the natural order. The ranch belonged to my beginning and would stay put. But a time of crisis came, for me and for the ranch, and I went back to it. And like the Chumash Indians who lived there first, I encountered certain powers that were in the wilderness; and they bore no relation to the familiar ones sufficient for human affairs. (Those were not good enough for what had to be done.) The Chumash knew this; faced with any crisis they called up their powers who then spoke through their wise people and artists to tell them the way to go. I was not an artist, nor did I feel especially wise, but somehow I knew I had to try. It was the only way I could make it work.

The real miracle was that so much land—five ranches totalling 39,000 acres—belonged to one family for more than a hundred years. The largest section, west of Santa Barbara, was approximately 25,000 acres and extended along the Pacific for twenty miles from Point Conception to five miles beyond Gaviota. In Spanish and Mexican days it was

called *La Nuestra Señora del Refugio* ("Our Lady of Refuge"). In my grandfather's and father's times it became known as the Santa Anita, because the old ranch headquarters was located at the Santa Anita Canyon, which was about a day's ride on horseback from either Point Conception or the Arroyo Hondo that marked its eastern boundary. But no matter what its name has been over the years, most people have called it "The Hollister Ranch." This was the ranch that determined my life. It is one of the last wild coastal tracts of that size between the Oregon border and Baja California.

"In wildness is the preservation of the world," Thoreau said. But when my father, John James Hollister, died in 1961,

the will and the way to keep that wildness died with him. It was no longer one man's prerogative. Nor, apparently, was it even a single family's. We were going to be forced to sell it, my brothers and cousins and I. All the land would have to go; all the ranch buildings, the stock, the equipment—every saddle, bridle, every stick and stone. It would have to be a clean sweep.

On the afternoon of his funeral we gathered to honor this man who had held such a legacy intact for the main part of his 91 years. All of us were deeply affected. Some were stunned by the prospect of loss; others gloated, contemplating cash and escape. We were bitterly divided, but none could deny the power of that land. The special, spiritually meaningful (and often destructive) impact of the ranch was obvious. I proved it by my behavior, as did the others. The fantastic beauty, the ruggedness, and the cruelty of the ranches touched us more deeply than we had suspected. We knew that even a place so beautiful could harbor feelings of fear, or revenge—even hatred.

In my own defense, however, I was trying to speak on behalf of an era now finished. The threatened loss of our ranches was not only a reflection of our ineptness and dissension in the last decade of the hundred years of family ownership; it was also a phenomenon of the times.

Ownership was the problem. But all the time in the background loomed the debatable questions: whether land can belong to anyone, or whether one belongs to the land. We had all shared in the glamour of immense, privately owned land. Whether earned or inherited, it was our mark of distinction.

My father rarely wore his *chapaderos*, and, to my knowledge, never used his silver-inlaid saddle or bridle; but our Mexican ranch hands knew him for what he was. They called him "El Patrón." All of us had been given a chance to live a part of history, to experience an era virtually extinct elsewhere in California.

In my generation we were seven. I was the only girl amidst three brothers and three cousins. My twin brother, Clinton, loved our land as I did but never realized the importance of its hold on him. My second brother, Joseph, also; but he died before its disposal was accomplished. My oldest brother, John James, Jr., and my three cousins, in the end, could not get past their anger—for my father had left me with the power to vote more than half the shares. I was to take my father's place—not his sons nor his nephews. My father must have known that I was as stubborn as he and would try to tackle the problems; and as the only woman I would be outside the male competition. But the outrage it caused only compounded the existing situation, and so the struggle began amongst the seven of us. It lasted until the ranches were finally sold in 1967.

*In 1868 my grandfather William Welles Hollister became sole
owner of the only Spanish land grant in the area; the others
were Mexican and more recent. He arranged for purchase of
a major part of* La Nuestra Señora del Refugio, *as the ranch
was officially called, from the Lobero family, who had bought
it from the Carrillos. Originally, it had been deeded to Cap-
tain Jose Francisco Ortega in recognition of his services on
the Portola expedition of 1769 (which led to the discovery of
San Francisco Bay).*

7

In the nineteenth century my grandfather and his partners, Albert and Thomas Dibblee, owned a vast empire of land northwest of Santa Barbara. When the partnership was dissolved, my grandfather's share was five large tracts arranged around what had been its heartland—the rich farmland. What was left for us was, however, more scenic, and contained the fossil deposits that eventually kept us solvent.

Our ranches then occupied much of the northwestern corner of Santa Barbara County. La Nuestra Señora del Refugio was unique in California; its southern boundary was the Pacific Ocean, because of the lie of the coast at that point. The Santa Ynez spur, which borders on the north, is an impassable wall of chaparral with boulders big as houses. This section of the range extends from Point Conception along the California coast in an easterly direction to the Arroyo Hondo and is interrupted only once by the Gaviota Pass. At least twenty deep canyons, with narrow ridges dividing them, flank the mountain range in a north/south direction and largely make up the big ranch. Huge, ancient, black-green oaks fill these canyons; in summer the hills and ridges are tawny gold, in winter emerald green.

Yet it seemed important that someone understand why love of land can transcend human love, as it did for my father and grandfather; and why others of my generation, who had turned against their heritage, were nonetheless caught and held by it, each in his own way.

Nevertheless, in the task of finding the meaning of our place it would be necessary to formulate a concept larger than the life of one family. It would have to be large enough to span the violence of elemental extremes and the unbelievably tentative gentleness that would too soon be destroyed.

Clearly, the beginning, as always, was the ranch itself, and its message came only when I was alone in that wilderness. There were unseen but potent voices asking to be recorded: bombardments of them, confused, groping, nearly always embarrassingly sentimental. But unruly as they were, the more they were honored the more they would reveal their secrets.

As I roamed the hills and mesas and canyons in a farewell to my wilderness home, I came to the most important conclusion of all: that I must go my own way, and go on. I would have to evolve by first sustaining the impact of those lands— and then, perhaps by speaking for them, ultimately be free of them.

Because of my compulsion to take notes, the medium must be language. And to find the telling words I would have to proceed blindly. I would have to sustain the chaos and the undifferentiated jumble of feelings turned loose. I would have to believe, as the Chumash did, that there were ordering forces in the offing.

With this in mind I began to write the Ranch Papers.

Without context, words and actions have no meaning at all.

Gregory Bateson *Mind and Nature*

CHAPTER ONE

The Falls

In June, after my father's death, I was at last free to roam the coast ranch—to look around in my own way. This first lonely visit was unannounced although I was virtually the head of the family by then. No one was there to meet me—not even the ranch hands. I had none of the honor and recognition given automatically to *El Patrón*. The ranch seemed deserted. I was being deliberately avoided.

Wandering aimlessly, I found myself walking into the canyon that stretched in back of the old family home. An unexpectedly peaceful feeling came over me. It came from the stillness under the great oaks. The disappointment at seeing no one quickly faded. At least the land was there to greet me.

I walked instinctively to where my twin brother and I had gone as small children. It was our outermost limit of adventure when we were little. Because our parents were too busy to concern themselves with us, we could mark our own boundaries. The place had become special long ago; it was ours, we had discovered it—the waterfall that spills over the great ledge of rock a mile or more into the canyon. It would be my objective that day as it had been in my childhood.

I went farther into Bulito Canyon along the dry creekbed where there were cattle trails under the dark ceiling of interlacing tree branches. It was cool and pleasant in the deep shade of the live oaks, and it gave me the brief chance to savor a past free from family turmoil. Our falls appeared around the bend. They were smaller and more intimate than I remembered. Water trickled down from a pool fed by a thin stream, which skipped down the rock face from far above, from a high ground of oaks and shrubs. The cattle had churned up the mud. When I sat on the sandstone, the silence came in force. It was an old friend from long ago and lifted my feelings of heaviness. It was good to be quiet, in spite of the thoughts and feelings that had piled up in the aftermath of my father's long life. To still them I deliberately called up memories that might point to what I needed to know and felt was asking to be known. I knew memories would focus me on what lay ahead. This land and my memories were inextricable.

Silence is another form of sound. I recalled how at times it rang in my ears, and I thought how as a child I had to listen carefully. We always stopped to listen. It had become a habit— no sound in the wild country was ever left uninterpreted.

The June quiet for the first time seemed different. It was not as I remembered it from earliest times—a caress, a great soft cloak drawn lightly around you. Instead it conveyed a sense of pressure. There was the suppression of sound that always happens when an intruder enters. I had never before noted the difference.

In the past, even when I walked into the dark wooded canyon as quietly as I could, I knew I would see nothing. It was no different this time. The place was apparently uninhabited, yet I had the feeling that many pairs of eyes were observing my slightest movement. I was right; I was being watched. From experience, too, I knew that once I sat quietly and waited long enough the whole place would come back to its busy, curious, noisy life—a life ordered within its disorder. Only the coyote, who follows like a dog, would never honor me by coming into view.

That day, after first settling in, only small alarms interrupted the stillness. I sat higher on the sandstone ledge to recollect a few of the conflicting feelings and to try to sort them with the help of nature's overall plan. This spot was a vantage point from which I could survey a fair distance down the creek and along the canyon flats to the reservoir. An overwhelming impulse to record what I was to see came over me.

Completely fitting the resolve I had made, it came from that vague earlier need to articulate what had been taken for granted all my life. I wanted to get some bearings from a sense of the totality that the ranch was, and especially to stop the unpleasant sense of floating in the vacuum that my father's death had left. There was, besides, an anticipation of overwhelming problems created by his long life; spanning the era of profitable cattle ranching and modern times when cattle no longer paid, we were faced with the need for radical changes in our operation.

Unexpectedly, giant frogs, which until then had been camouflaged against the sandstone, flopped from out of nowhere into the pool. Deep, hollow and refreshing, their sounds were clean against the still water as they echoed against the sheer wall. I counted them as they jumped—one after the other, as though clocked by an unseen presence. They were part of my settling further into the scene.

Several blushing, red-headed linnets, otherwise known as house finches, and a small speckled thrush, with light spots on an earth-brown body, appeared in the circle of the falls. The sound of a relaxed trickle of water came from the moss-slicked rock face. The buzz of linnets' wings echoed briefly against the high semicircle of overhead sandstone that looked more like hardened mud. A canyon wren appeared, tiny and perfect. He flipped his tail like a pointer, this way, then that, his head low on his tip-tilted body as though by habit he was prone to look under things. His dainty song penetrated the silence. For the moment my troubles would have to wait. Looking around I saw orderly rows of delicately shining, black-stemmed maidenhair ferns lodged in the seeping dampness of the green moss at the base of the wall. Reflecting brightly in the water, they made a broad fringe. Two poplar branches rubbed together in the slight breeze. The familiarity of the sounds successfully merged the immediacy of the moment with a distant past.

I heard the liquid *shreeee* of a rufous-sided towhee on the opposite bank. Dressed up in black, orange and white, he looked at me out of startling red eyes. From the distance came the sad undulating message of a lonely mourning dove. I was becoming one with these creatures. The far past continued blending into the present; it would not be put down. Old reflexes had been lying there waiting.

Belonging at last brought with it a peaceful feeling. Experiencing the vast world of sounds and sights that had always been there, lodged in the outer reaches of my awareness, was like coming home. I wondered why I had never before consciously focused on this place. It then occurred to me that, as children, we were never encouraged to report on our day's activities. We were unaccustomed to putting our experiences into words. Instead we had indulged (or escaped into?) secret lives of our own, and were filled with happenings left undigested deep down in us. We had been in a constant state of uncommunicated excitement. It was as though day after day we had what hunters call "buck fever"—the tremor that overtakes the novice when he is at last faced by his quarry. Our quarry was the unexpected minute-to-minute, day-to-day manifestation of nature. But, much later, I discovered that we were the hunted and nature was the hunter.

The gentle wind at the falls rustled the reeds and the poplar leaves as though they were paper. The questioning of the linnets was loud against the mud walls for the moments before they let loose songs, urgent and eager, from deep in their throats. I, the intruder, was at last pronounced harmless. Their songs—increasingly bold, magnified rich and immanent because of the magic enclosure—became persistent, even driven. They took over the falls. When they flew their melodies were synchronized with their wingbeats.

That June day I looked into the natural surroundings of my childhood that remained unchanged. I was lucky. In an era of rapid change, that is a rare privilege. Had the opportunity been otherwise, the undertones and overtones evolved during the impressionable childhood years would have been lost for good. More often than not, when coming to a place for the first time in one's adult years, it is impossible to grasp more than what can be seen on the surface.

Perhaps it was just as well that as children we could not articulate our earliest experiences. Had we been encouraged to do so, we might have dissipated them, and they would not have remained in our memories to be enriched by the long view. There is something intriguing about a secret liaison. If we are favored, and youth roots down in untouched wilderness it can flower, finally, in old age. On the other hand, had the Chumash been honored, I at least might have been saved the task of trying to understand why so many of us were entrapped by scenes like this one.

My mother made feeble attempts to focus our attention on civilization by reading fairy tales to us. But the fairytale animals had been anthropomorphized beyond recognition and, for the most part, we were bored with them. Animals do talk—but not like human beings. Our experience of animals was far too real and exciting for us to fall for those fabricated versions. We knew better. Animal stories were anemic compared with the real wild world.

The more I thought about it, the luckier I felt in my silence and in the forced silence of a place no one knew. Prehistoric animals have been discovered, preserved in ice, with every detail intact. In much the same fashion, the sounds and sights coming to my attention had been preserved in my childhood psyche. I was beginning to be glad of my neglected past self and its silent pact with nature.

The thin whir of an unseen hummingbird threaded through these thoughts at the falls. The flutter of a curious olive-backed thrush ushered in a momentary silence that was broken only by a bee's steady drilling at an orange flower in the rock barely over my shoulder. Then, keyed below the others was the tiny scolding of a bushtit. Over all soared the wail of a lone killdeer landing at the nearby reservoir. His sharp ocean cry resounded oddly in this inland quiet. In and out of these sounds were the monotonous demands for food coming from a young linnet. Sounds, thoughts, memories and old reflexes intermingled.

By then I was scribbling hard in order to record every happening. Something told me not to leave out the smallest detail. In time I would find a clue to it all, but now it was impossible to know what took precedence over what.

A small, plump Oregon junco with a black head and neck, russet back, white showing in his tail when he flew, rummaged in the nearby bushes; as if he felt me too near his nest—although it was late in the season for nests. In a tree high up was a downy woodpecker with a tiny trip-hammer in his head, his cap bright red, his body black with thin parallel white stripes. For such a small jaunty, gaudy jailbird he had a rasping voice. He bobbed over and around and under an oak limb, playing his highest notes fast and loud. There was no doubt about his nest. In the distance, there was the less alarmed *arrrrrrita* of another woodpecker. The sudden, all-out movements of the creature struck a note, and something in his thrust, and precision, his all-or-nothing manner touched me. Doubts, hesitancy, divided mind and lapse of attention do not exist in nature as they do in us. The slightest pause invites death. In my inmost being there was a response and I came to know more about that, too, as the months passed by.

A flycatcher soundlessly feathering his wings in midair in pursuit of an insect came to rest again and again on a thin vine hanging precariously from the rim. The last of the season's cliff swallows, as silent and erratic as bats, flew out to the reservoir to pluck mud for the nests they were building

neatly into the hollows of the wall. A covey of quail burst out of the sage below me, skimming over it to another feeding ground. A roadrunner, with his long snakelike neck and brilliant, yellow, seemingly lidless eyes, sped past characteristically, without sound, exactly following a narrow trail as though his life depended on it. I knew how he swallowed poisonous snakes, and I thought he had not completely lost the effect of his inherited reptilian outline. After all, he had begun to look like his present self only at the turn of the Cenozoic era.

Firmly settled into my favorite childhood place—a small, special place outside of time—I was again open to conflicting questions. Would the part of me connected to this place now emerge, with something to say? Could the years of my twenties, thirties, forties, spent in cities, be bridged over, back to my childhood, by means of the small beachhead my notes were becoming? Or would I find out much later it was the other way around? Would I find that my middle age had been an unreal city existence and that my reality was still in the distant past?

There are two kinds of people: those who can live without wild things and those who cannot.

Aldo Leopold *A Sand County Almanac*

CHAPTER TWO

The San Augustine Canyon

THE HORSES WERE SCATTERED, grazing in the field, and it was already on into the morning. I had to ride Old Roan through them on the way to the San Augustine Canyon. Muffled by their long hair, they looked almost as if they were wearing fur coats. Patches of hair on their muzzles had forgotten to stop growing. These long chin whiskers and the shaggy hair on their undersides and legs gave them a woolly prehistoric look, the stance of their ancestors in the Lascaux caves. Some giant hand could have sketched them against the pasture, but for me they were an assurance that all was well in my small world.

The horses crowded around us. Their curiosity overcame their instinct to flee—and that made them a nuisance. But I thought: What if they were all on a rampage and I were on foot?

The horses immediately started to follow us to the gate at the end of the field in the Canyon of *Las Agujas* (Spanish for "needles"). The cold was in them; they needed to run, but they kept clustering in a wide circle around us. They had no intention of being caught. Like flags, their ears and tails were up. They trotted back and forth along the fence. Several times, they were close enough to bolt through the gate I had opened. Old Roan got into the act. More like a colt than an old horse, he put up his head and tail and swung around at the end of his long rein. He whinnied hopefully. Cattle and horses behave like that before a storm. Their playfulness seems to come out of an instinctual need to prepare for oncoming wet and cold.

I had picked the San Augustine Canyon this morning for no particular reason; I was in the mood to drift and be drawn into the quiet depths of the back country—to the boundaries of my adolescent past.

A cold wind was in charge. Within the mass of small, dark, blue-green malva leaves by the gate at the canyon end of the field, little faces watched the sun climb heavily as it does in winter. Unlike the grass, each leaf shuddered slightly. The wild mustard, faintly cast in yellow, seemed already to be hinting at the rich outpouring of its flowers. The light was surprisingly white considering it was not yet noon; and the signs of storm had disappeared, except for a slight dampness in the north wind.

Past the first low ridge, fat brown birds—a rare species of brown towhee—half ran, half flew back and forth through the strands of rusty barbed wire fence in the brush. Reluctant to leave the ground, they raced ahead of Old Roan, barely safe from his forefeet. Their tails, frantic rudders to their careening, showed rusty undersides. Noiseless, they wriggled their way effortlessly, in spite of their size, through intricate places in the thick brush. I wondered if their color scheme, fitting perfectly the browns of Southern California, preserved them here in such great numbers. A reddish monarch butterfly sailed conspicuously over their heads, picking up the air currents. A single lonely survivor of the rains, he was barely airborne upon thin wings, which were ragged and faded.

Through the gate in Las Agujas Canyon grew a fine weed. It formed a winter turf, spongy and thick enough for my horse to walk on without leaving a hoof mark. Young leaves of a purple thistle hugged the ground. White speckles paled their green. They were all innocence for those who have never encountered them in their prickly middle age—they could have accounted for the canyon's name. Arroyo willows with minute leafy hands, turned over and grayed in the sun by the wind, formed a thicket nearby. Tucked inside were their silky catkins that looked like tiny cockades. The poison oak was barely emerging: red and angry on its long, thin, rigid, swelling stems—positively phallic in its aggressiveness.

The deadly nightshade was clothed in undistinguished lavender flowers. Friends and foes gathered unobtrusively to make a whole, having arrived on time, that day, the year before and—I would like to believe—forever.

Old Roan scrambled to the ridge along the top of the San Augustine watershed where the unused jeep road led to its headwaters. In their pursuit of insects, western flycatchers in yellow and gray somersaulted from the dilapidated rusty wire bordering the road, a fence that was built at the turn of the century. One, coming to rest, braced itself in a delicate balancing act on the only mustard stalk left from the year before.

What was not there mattered even more: the absence of signs of human life, except for some evidence of our agricultural efforts. (Only the mesas could be cultivated.) But what about the 10,000, maybe 50,000 years of Chumash culture that had been totally obliterated?

What were the Chumash Indians like? So little is known about them. My parents, belonging to the generation that despised Indians, left me to find out in my middle age that certain Spanish padres, a Lieutenant Fages on the Portola expedition, and Richard Dana, a century later, had, in their diaries, given them some of their due. In my fantasy I let their shapes come into focus among the manzanita; soft dark forms, a copper color, standing out against the white shale. They were solemnly going about their business and like their surroundings, that quiet morning, a graceful, gentle heritage.

The Spanish, the least harsh of the invaders, I learned, forced on them their way of life. Possibly they were threatened by the Indian's natural dignity. Perhaps they could not stand his "otherness." More likely underlying self-doubts were constellated by the aboriginal aloofness. Whatever the reason, religious prejudice caused the Spanish to impose on the Indians the tyranny of highly militant beliefs unsuited to them. For "men of nature," engrossed in their natural cyclic environment, the Spanish belief was far too evolved from natural roots. It took the heart out of people whose psychic doors were ajar, who were vulnerable and open to the healing nature of seasonal beginnings and endings.

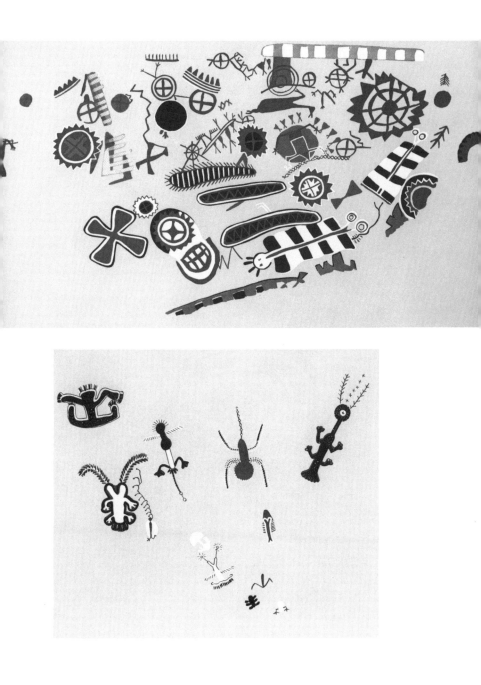

The Chumash lacked immunity to the European diseases and died by the hundreds. Those who survived became peons in the imported Spanish social structure; they became the labor force needed to build towns and rambling estancias. By the time of my father's generation, most of them had been "reduced" (a mission term for conversion) to a faceless, anonymous, degenerated stratum of society. Identified with nature and therefore lacking the kind of willpower we know, they *could not serve masters whose roots were elsewhere and whose god had long before lost connection with nature.*

After the Spanish came the Yankees, with visions of Eldorado. Followers of revolutions and democracy, they dreamed of paradise on earth, of material ease and luxury. They did not see the fantastic beauty of the wilderness laid out for them. Buying out the Spaniards, by then under the Mexican flag (and perpetuating the tragedy), they accelerated the demise of the Indian population. My grandfather was one of them; through him I share the blame. Still later and in other parts of California, the surviving Indians were herded off to ghetto-like reservations—their tribal differences totally disregarded, their beliefs and rituals systematically taken from them.

Our own roots were thereby permanently cut.

Old Roan clattered up the white shale road to a higher point in full view of the upper San Augustine. It was a lonely canyon with ridges outstretched like arms. The sun filled every crevice, making the green speak out—the range grass, the heavy young mustard, the gray-green chaparral in the rocks and the dark oaks. The small valley had its own separate small sun cozily dedicated to its contours. There was the soft expectant reticence of protected places: a deity was in residence.

It was intruded upon by the noise of Old Roan's hooves echoing against the rocks and his impatience with the view. I knew his wild associates, well out of sight, were silently observing us.

No matter how plentiful, wildlife in these places seeks cover at the slightest interruption. All activity stops. Nothing is taken for granted in the wilderness. Like the wildlife, and certainly the Chumash, we who were also reared here never let a sound or unfamiliar movement pass without questioning its source. There was always an explanation. Imagine a similar attitude in sound-infested cities! Think of the potential for discoveries, the glut of undigested data! But one must also remember that there are those few who, through the centuries, have applied the same sensitive curiosity. The resulting discrimination was responsible for our own fantastic (if not exactly ideal) evolution.

Curiosity, taking nothing for granted and pushing for an explanation essential to survival in the wilderness, places us in the broadest stream of life. These instinctive habits, accompanied by sympathetic understanding, should have connected us to our indigenous predecessors—the Chumash Indians—and should have prevented their extermination. In turn, they could have enhanced our inspiration in the broad evolutionary terms we needed by means of their wilderness integrity. What might have been if we had come to this coast with more humility and understanding!

Farther along the trail, stranger reactions began to register. What I saw was almost entirely for my own pleasure. It was a private affair like so much of nature, which thrives in secret.

It is said that isolation threatens one's sanity, and casualties do occur in these out-of-the-way places. On the other hand, life geared to the isolation of nature has some of the magic of a dream that can be told. It is subliminal, having, in a sense, autonomy. It reads its own barometers. The aboriginals know about this deep level of existence: the mysterious cyclical participation with nature.

Thoughts continued to crowd and proliferate. I was again focusing on what had been relevant and in proportion when I was a child. Returning to my earliest impressions, I wanted to link them to what I know of so-called civilized life.

"Civilized" societies are also cyclic but mainly in a long-term historically recorded sense—too long for populations to learn about war, overpopulation, scarcity, even overabundance. Only individuals register and honor the anniversaries of their personal experiences, such as births, marriages, and deaths. The natural sensitivity that primitive peoples had toward nature is lost. Civilized people no longer experience nature deeply enough for them to deal with crises adequately.

They seem instead destined in the long run to destroy themselves. Nature's cyclic death and rebirth life patterns are discarded. With modern "push-button" society (and the equivalent in earlier societies that prospered on the labor of conquered peoples) civilized people have been too protected from the natural realities of life.

Had my family for instance applied the Indian cyclic attitude, we would have had a better chance to deal with hazards that plagued us. We could have taken the droughts in our stride. We could at least have reduced our distress had we looked on the years of abundance and scarcity, like the Indians, as only aspects of a cosmic game of chance—thus lifting the issues out of our personal ego spheres. Long-term planning might have come out of such an attitude.

In modern psychology repeated happenings seen as motifs are now known as archetypal. (A rediscovery of psychical nature prompted certain people to make this discovery.) It is our way of expressing what the Chumash had for centuries lived as rituals and legends; these rituals expressed (and kept within manageable limits) the myriads of recurring phenomena they had to deal with.

Had the circumstances been otherwise, had our family been allowed to keep our lands, childhood impressions of the land could have remained as undetected underpinnings, sustaining us for the rest of our lives. It would not have been necessary to feel the pain of reviving them only to help me to fit more comfortably into the high and dry cities—to help me to live. In addition, I might have remained in my unquestioned symbiotic relationship with nature.

By civilized standards, my twin brother and I had been swallowed up in the vastness of the ranch during our most formative years. It was as though we had grown up in a trance, like sleepwalkers, muffled by the land's huge embrace. We appeared to be slow and unbelieving. People we encountered were impatient with us, not knowing we needed time to consider all sides. Like the wild life around us, we weighed, listened, checked and considered at length before we moved into unfamiliar situations. Conservatism for the sake of self-preservation was the key to understanding the natural level on which we lived.

The fact that we destroyed the Indians has been destructive for us. We lacked even the structuring influence of the simplest customs and rituals normally available to Indian children. We lived in a fantastic but real world of our own discovery: square miles of impassable terrain, wild cattle threatening on the trail, single coyotes caterwauling like a pack, pumas screaming, storms felling giant oaks, washouts that marooned us for days, wildfires that lasted weeks and scorched whole mountain ranges. We were lost in the constant turmoil where too much was happening to make it our own, in a form that could be communicated. The daily episodes of birth and death strike nakedly the inmost being of a child. The devastating defeats were more often than not experienced in solitude, yet somehow had to be met. Conquests big and small had to be experienced without qualification. Insects, birds and animals ordinarily relegated to books were vibrant and alive before us. Personifications were not invoked.

Local gossip became fact, and hearsay beyond what we actually observed became scientific report. No one had the time to set us straight. Evenings, traditionally the time for satisfying curiosity, sharing knowledge, and making human connection, were wiped out by the fatigue that comes from long days of the utmost physical exertion in clean air.

The odds were either against us or for us, depending on our outlook. But we were stuck in a kind of inarticulateness for most of our lives. I remember well how often in our childhood our elders shouted at us: "Open your mouth when you talk!"

Nevertheless, we enjoyed the snobbery of "first comers." We had our own kind of assurance and natural dignity, though it was so impersonal a brand that few people recognized it as such. "Unrelated," some people called us. "Gone native," others said. To my mind, however, we were part of a small, special elite that only raw country produces—when it

does not destroy. Quirks, meannesses, indignities and super-
ficialities have no place where the wilderness dominates. We
were fortunate in this.

Considering we were fated to lose our context, it might
have been easier if we *had* been reared in "civilization,"
where the burden of what is lacking in one is carried by another. We would not have been faced with the need to struggle painfully to extricate ourselves from the land. Nor would
we have inherited so large an assignment: our god was nature, not a deity reduced to the likeness of man. Our model
was more inclusive and harder to live by. Fortunately, at my
age, 58, with the land as it was years ago and with the help
of my horse, I could still dip into the rich reservoir of impressions. Like submerged strata of life these impressions were
waiting as though they had only just happened and had surfaced intact.

From the high point overlooking the upper San Augustine Canyon, I could see a bare section of the great sandstone barrier, which is made up of giant white slabs tipping back to describe a parabola high over the ocean. The gigantic sand and rock strata—Vaqueros Sands—were softened to intimacy by the tender young sage. This was another of nature's contrasts, not opposites, for she makes whole statements, not partial ones, as we seem fated to do.

A great live oak stood at the narrows formed by the sandstone through which the creek flowed. Its old age was evident in the size of its giant trunk, although its overall mass had been ruthlessly reduced. Close up, new leaves clustered brightly among the dead-looking wood ends. Clothed in new light-green leaves, the whole tree shone in contrast to the black-green of another oak almost touching on its right. This neighbor seemed to have fared better. From the abundance of the new growth in the first tree, one might guess it had lost its foliage during the preceding summer and was having to make a fresh start. The luxuriance of this old tree's leafy growth was more than likely heralding its last effort. The purpose of its exuberance might have been to ensure the ultimate transition—the show of strength needed for the big push.

I felt the promise of a rebirth. Rebirth for a tree, perhaps, but not for the Chumash, who counted less than the oaks. (There were, for instance, almost no Chumash names of employees listed on papers submitted to court by my grandmother's ranch managers during the settling of my grandfather's will.)

I rode past the sandstone boulders through the barrier wall and along the trail where it is forced to give way to the rough contours of more sandstone scattered beyond. There I found the thick, stiff growth of many varieties of shrubs. Typically, I also found two kinds of oaks like the ones I first encountered. I stopped deliberately to take them in. Some seemed to have gotten their start in good times, and grown fast. Clean-limbed, vigorous and untraumatized, they possessed the tall, straight bearing associated with privilege. Despite their size, they suggested youth; their single straight trunks told me they started in wet years when the deer, having enough vegetation to feed on, did not munch them to the ground. These oaks, their trunks topped by massive, dark-green leafy branches, are without history, although they may be among the most ancient.

Other ancient oaks, with bifurcated battered trunks and twisting limbs, must have started in years of low rainfall when all the grass eaters would have relished them. Initially cut back to the level of the ground, they seemed to have compensated by sending up two, sometimes three trunks rather than one. They somehow had to lower their centers of gravity, probably in order to endure. Individual events in the form of droughts, winds, fires, floods and needs of predators are written into the contorted, ancient limbs and gnarled, misshapen trunks.

An oak in the San Augustine Canyon supported a great dragon of a limb bent so low it lay full length on the ground. The limb's great weight, or some elemental force, must have brought it down long ago. Small leafy branches at its outer end turned up healthily. According to one botanist, the low-lying feature is a sign of the tree's great age: perhaps two hundred years, he said. Oaks sometimes endure the worst conditions. Other times, with a touchiness hard to believe, they topple over in the dead of a soundless night, and the heavy thud can be heard for miles. Some oaks start on a simple course and then, for no apparent reason, alter radically. Another in the San Augustine had a girth high up on its trunk that greatly exceeded its base.

In the deeper, narrower and darker part of the same canyon there was still another oak I had overlooked all those years. Its biggest, blackest limb twisted around at the point where it emerged from the trunk, looking as if a huge hand had taken hold of it and turned it halfway around on itself. The folds literally formed a prehistoric reptilian eye. It had the half-conscious vigilance characterisitc of the reptile whose eyes are never closed. Sleepily, wisely, critically and eternally, it watched. The great limb actually breathed, and in this observation I was no different from the primitives. They certainly felt as I did before their gods and their tree and water spirits were taken from them.

The limb extended clumsily out to join the tree's perimeter as though to be part of the tree's fulfillment. Its length and weight should have crashed it to the ground. As with oaks everywhere, its smaller rotting branches looked ready to fall, dangerous to anything passing below. I somehow knew they would all be there a year later, looking as precarious as ever and surrounded by young, strong trees arbitrarily laid low. It was as if they had not yet received time's signal.

One undoubtedly notes the overtones of life in an extra-sensory way only when they have meaning in terms of one's own life, when there is an inner need for a vague notion to push its way into consciousness. Or, when one unknowingly takes up where the Chumash left off. I was content in my preoccupation with these overbearing tree shapes. Far away from distracting environments, one is allowed these privileges. My sensitivity to them needed no justification.

Given a wilderness to steep in, elements within us ripen and tend to find a sympathetic outer focus. We can revert to what our primitive predecessors took for granted in their empathy with nature, but first we must turn away from the philosophical search for meaning, expressed in the repeated cultural struggle for completion.

Nevertheless, a niggling thought could not be put down: did we, who were conditioned during childhood years in a broad, wild isolation, only *borrow* a sense of completeness? This is something civilization does not talk about. Did my brother and I get our sense of self-containment from the wholeness of the land around us? Or were we bound and hopelessly stuck in the subcultural layer of those earliest of early humans? I like to think that we started from a deeper psychic level than my civilized associates and could be the richer for such a beginning (that is, assuming we finally, totally filled in the extensive gap created by premature efforts to adapt to city and group life; I, for instance, was sent to boarding school at the age of eight with only vacations on the ranch from then on).

The more I looked, the more I saw that each great oak was not only individual and unique but was literally beckoning with a message for me. The oaks were frantically calling my attention. *There was no time to lose.* An articulation of what they stood for was long overdue.

The Chumash were still drifting as ghosts in my mind's half-light. At the beginning of their history, they had been an Oak Grove People. Their remains were found by archaeologists at high coastal elevations among traces of now extinct prehistoric oak forests. They certainly must have felt the magic—felt the oak images stirring within them, evoking the corresponding spirits.

Old Roan pulled at his bit. The oaks were an unchallenged part of his life; my need to record them in my notes only prolonged the time for turning back and he was impatient. Pawing the ground, he made my scribbles almost illegible.

A sweet song, its source kept secret by the protecting shrubs, came from among the oaks. The song was brief, because of our intrusion, yet true to itself. It could have come down the centuries as images of stars come to us preserved intact in their light years. It was a lovely reminder of the great age of this coast and the faithful flow of life since the beginning of time. The white-flowered mountain mahogany stood with its clusters of miniature petals around tiny buff-colored

centers. Stiff gray leaves on stiffer scratchy branches protected the frail flowers.

The swelling north wind, channeled down the canyon in
prolonged gusts, softened the cold. Listening closely I could
hear how the stronger gusts were laced into the faint ones. In
that cool, impartial air, velvet warm red manzanita branches
caught my attention, and I impulsively reached out to touch
them. Even in their small scale, their twisting showed the

years as the oaks showed their centuries. These interlocking stretches of time (short lives and long lives intertwining) are so much a part of untouched wilderness.

High up the steep slope at the trail's edge, among the scrub oaks, were clusters of prickly phlox facing into the winter sun. A few star-shaped succulents had braved the sandstone. Many signs of new growth brightened the sticky dark-green monkey flower shrubs, readying them for the long hot dry summer.

The future plays a big part in the early spring. (The Chinese Yang is in the Yin.) Its suggestion and promise touch me more than full-blown spring. It is the one moment of the year when last year's dead stalks can still be seen. The leached range grasses are grayed and flattened, and a few dead oak leaves still cling. Early spring also offers bits of color: single grass blades of piercing green, carpets of fine needlepoint green and quarter-way-to-bursting buds that guarantee a luxurious overabundance to come later. This is the season when you have the whole year in your grasp. The beginning of spring touches you where, in old age, you need reassurance—a feeling of past, present and future, a kind of timelessness.

On the north side of the sandstone ledges were intriguing shapes: large and small caves carved out by the prevailing north wind. Characteristically, those hidden places harbor nothing, not even the sticks and small rubbish of the tough wood rats. The constant cold north wind there discourages warm-blooded life.

The sandstone begins where the good range grass, growing out of the black soil, stops. The white shale jeep road, descending into the San Augustine, flows openly and gently along the creek, eventually leading up to it. This year the yearling Hereford heifers stuck it out there until the grass was gone. They had already cropped it to the ground, particularly near the water, and unless there is more rain they will be forced to graze beyond the ledges where the grass is tall and watery, and where the sunlight is reduced by the narrowing canyon. Their centuries-long conditioning in the lush green pastures of England make Herefords slow to leave flat places, unlike the deer and wild Mexican cattle that graze on the move, clipping little by little over a large area. The wilder the grazing animal, it seems, the more it keeps in motion to guard against detection and, inadvertently, the more it preserves a balanced vegetation.

The black soil below the ledge was adobe, and it "crawled." The fence-line built by the Chinese in my grandfather's time, leaning tipsily on the ridge, was proof. "It gallops," they used to say. Beyond the barrier, the earth was clearly a yellow clay. But adobe is, by definition, clay. The black soil that dries to a soft gray is the kind the Spaniards mixed with straw for their adobe houses. The yellow stuff is something else that would serve a sculptor's needs. Cracks had already dried into the yellow soil in spite of the recent rain. They formed a capillary system gracefully sketched around a few main arteries on the banks of the old jeep road.

Young gray-green sage grew soft and fuzzy on the edge of the trail. In each spring, it is like a sea of minute, delicate green feather dusters. I am always oblivious of the sticky branches until they catch me in the leg as I ride through. The softness and color of this sage is hard to convey. Yet, without a description of the sage, how can one be talking about California?

Listening and savoring observations as I rode along made me realize how objective science (botanical, biological, zoological, mythological, even archaeological) might have freed my twin brother and me long ago, as it does in old evolved and established cultures. But I also wondered if we would have participated in the same sort of love affair that the aborigines had with their surroundings. Knowledge supersedes impression. Naming relegates nature to the world of books, experts, and authorities. It dilutes the immediacy of the experience.

Oak groves darkened the upper part of the San Augustine. Where they met the steepening sides of the canyon, they were evenly trimmed to the height of a cow's lifted muzzle.

Branches below the muzzle-line were worn smooth from the cattle scratching themselves.

Oaks higher up were stunted by harsher conditions. Life against the mountains had condensed and gnarled them. The cattlemen still ride these canyons. Tall in the saddle—as the storybooks describe—they do not deign to step on the ground if they can help it. They are unlikely to be bothered with the fascination of such a place. They ride along, their horses clattering through the boulders, getting on with the job, feeling nothing, only noting if the cattle are there—or possibly a deer, even a coyote or a bobcat. They never feel the need to report what they see. Like their cattle, they are unselfconscious parts of the place. Encapsulated by the round of seasons, they do not make history as we know it, and are the better for not being tempted into egoistic thought, even when they are innately capable of it. They never have to fall short of simple acceptance. Aloofness and disdain, stemming from shyness, make them natural aristocrats of that domain.

We came to the end of the canyon, where it abuts against the foothills of the Santa Ynez range and then disappears into impassable rock and chaparral. The only signs of life were brief and accidental. The absence of cattle tracks indicated that they did not like it here, though the site offered protection from the persistent cold north wind. I felt shadows where nothing moved and imagined dark forms in the dense thickets and among the giant boulders. In spite of the loneliness, and silence and remoteness, I was not alone. The eeriness was disconcerting; it whispered of things beyond the senses. The little place literally reverberated with unanswerable questions. The voices were everywhere. It was in the ever-so-slight wind, the almost imperceptible movement of a branch, the leaf that flicked its way to the ground and the few rasping shouts of a scrubjay that echoed among the rocks. It could have been the home of a friendly resident spirit unaccustomed to being disturbed; but any spirit is a little upsetting. For that reason I turned for home with some relief. The feeling was emphasized by Old Roan's quickened pace and alerted ears.

Each of the five smaller ranches of my father's day had a place name descriptive of location or character. One named Sal Si Puedes *("escape if you can") appears on maps as* Salsipuedes. *It was once a swampy marsh; now it has 7000 acres of rich crop lands and groves of moss-covered oaks on its open range. Las Cruces, named for a crossroads, borders on the upper end of the Gaviota Pass. The map shows the diamond-shaped ranch balanced on its southern point where two highways converge—Route 101 from northern California, Route One from the coast—the same point where Spanish coach roads joined. One can still see there the remains of the stagecoach adobe inn where fresh horses were provided, before the railroad was built. Las Cruces, nearly as big as Salsipuedes, was bitter cold in winter and steaming hot in summer. It sustained extensive orchards on its rich bottomland.*

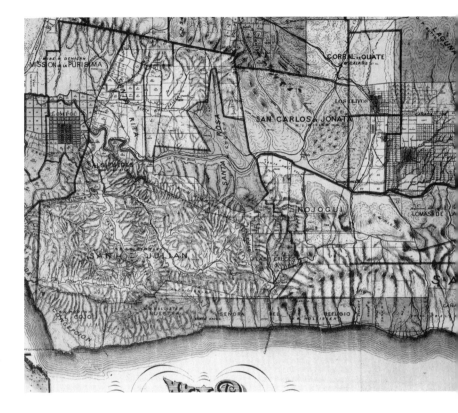

La Gaviota, *on the coast east of the Gaviota Pass, was given the Spanish name for "seagull" by Fremont's soldiers during the U.S.-Mexican War. It was slightly smaller than Las Cruces. The* Winchester, *west of Santa Barbara, was named for my grandfather's family doctor and had 1000 acres, its comfortable family home surrounded by walnut and avocado orchards. The* Santa Anita, *lying on the only east-west coastal strip of California, extended from the Gaviota Pass to Point Conception and was the most extensive ranch of the lot— about 18,000 acres. Santa Anita Canyon was located at its center. It was kept moist by frequent summer fogs, its rangeland supporting a large herd of white-faced Hereford cattle.*

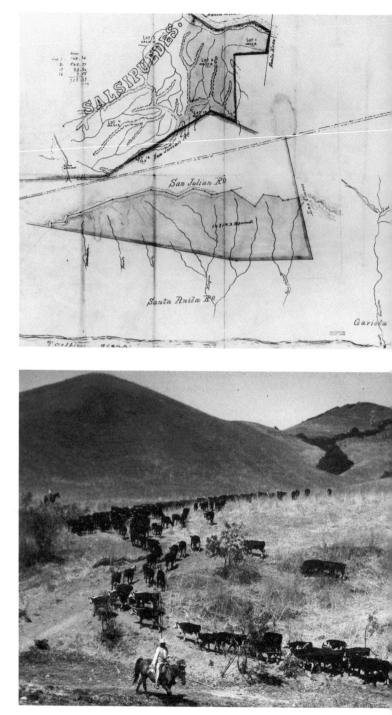

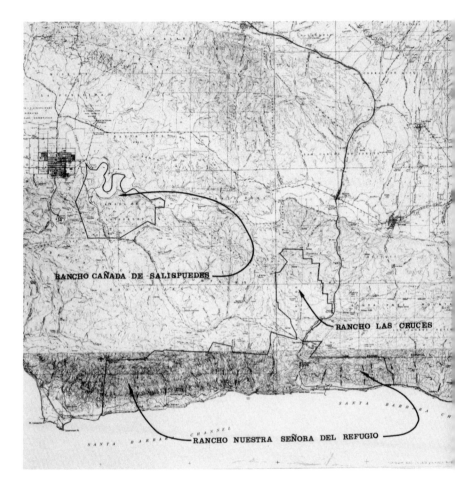

RANCHO CAÑADA DE SALISPUEDES

RANCHO LAS CRUCES

RANCHO NUESTRA SEÑORA DEL REFUGIO

43

45

A beautiful country, a warm climate, an abundance of grain and cattle—and nothing else.

Doña Concepciòn Arguello 1806
cited in *California—a Place, a People, a Dream:
A Journey Through California History*

CHAPTER THREE

The Corrals

IN THE AFTERNOON my bones were wearing through to the saddle, a familiar experience from years of riding dawn to dusk. But in my preoccupation I welcomed the sensation as a token of the reality of the day.

There had been, indeed, a driving need to prove the uniqueness of this country. My fate was that deeply involved.

A sparrow hawk sat on one of the series of high poles that carried the power line for water development. The hawk fell into flight as we approached, forming a desultory half circle only to straighten out and gain a perch on the next pole. The flight pattern was so characteristic that I wondered if sparrow hawks all over California have been conditioned in their habits by power poles. In the past I had not noticed the special qualities of these small hawks. The geometric designs of their faces were almost Aztecan.

Underfoot on the white jeep road were small, round, faintly colored stones churned up from the sandstone by the cattle and lying loose in the dust; others barely showed in the hardened sand walls. They are part of an aeons-old aggregate made up of river pebbles originally gathered and rolled by ancient torrents and deposited far from their source. These troubled formations are probably the result of prehistoric deluges cascading from the retreat of the last glacier. Significantly, the Oak Grove People were driven at that time to high ground. Something in the small polished stones pulled me off my horse to fill my pockets guiltily, like a small boy who tries to bring home eggs from a wild nest. (A small girl would not

be tempted in that way, because females tend to preserve life.) I was drawn equally to the simultaneous qualities of newness and infinite age that showed in the clean shapes.

Maybe the egglike stones were awakening feelings of the beginning of all things asleep deep inside me. Whatever the explanation, I felt a twinge of embarrassment at the thought of being seen gathering them. Nor did Old Roan's questioning help. One's potential self-consciousness can be acutely vulnerable to an old horse's quizzical look, especially when the deepest psychic stratum is touched at his level.

The creek in San Augustine Canyon sporadically went underground. Millions of years ago, during the ice age, creek beds on this coast were three hundred feet below their present course, in order to meet the sea. Since then, soft silt has filled in to meet the present level, making way for the underground channeling.

Where the creek water surfaced, its cheerful monologue could be heard as far as the sled road high on the ridge. The sound was always pleasing, but hard to describe. No wonder the Zen masters instruct their pupils to grasp the sound of a running stream if they wish to find the secret of life. Numerous rocks, broken-off outcroppings washed white by the rains, lay in the long, heavily grassed hillside crease where the fronting hills dipped to the mesa. It was as though they had been arbitrarily picked up and dumped by an elemental force. I could have sworn they had not been there before that day. The coastal strip out of which the rocks came is officially classified as Monterey Shale. The local geologists call it slumping soil. The light brown chert from this stratum was used by the Chumash Indians for tools, arrow and spearheads.

When grandfather died in 1886, my grandmother inherited the ranches—and soon put them up for sale. The isolation had no appeal for her. Like my mother, she had been a city product. But my father stepped in and reversed her plans. The grass in the Santa Anita Canyon, he said, made the decision; it was tall enough to tie across the saddle, and land that produced grass like that could make a good living—the heavy debts incurred by my grandfather's important but unprofitable civic ventures (and his family's extravagances) could be paid off, given time. The Santa Anita was the ranch that determined my life. For my father's generation it became a retreat because of its protective contours—and because it was nearly inaccessible. Its location suited my father, his taciturn nature a match for its solitude. And because of this wild isolation the ranch was always the beginning of things for me; to this day, as it was when I was a little girl, my creative energies are loosed the moment I set foot there.

Changing inner needs drive one to see differently at different times. One can overlook rocks like these one day, or see them as lifeless objects when in someone's company, and another time, alone, find them reverberating with overtones, like auras. Drawn to them this time, I felt I was at last witnessing their whirling molecules.

A lowly pile of rocks—significance laid upon significance since the earth's cooling—possessed emerging shapes with suggested prehistoric forms. Fantasies evolved out of spontaneous, vague impressions. Ancient dream memories were stirred by phantoms rising from the molds and lines of compression. Object after object took on a vibrance as though having a life of its own. Nature was speaking for herself. Facts were not allowed to spoil the impressions of a whole day alone. They had been tossed out in the manner of the rocks, tossed on the slope. The spirit was aloof.

Where the canyon leads out to the mesas there is a eucalyptus grove marking the site of the old San Augustine ranch headquarters. The grove dominates a broad, black stretch of bottomland in the lower part of the canyon. Elephant grass and alfalfa were barely holding their own. They were all that was left of early efforts to shorten the long dry summer gap and provide vitamin A for the cattle.

The grove was designed to protect ranch buildings from the winds in the interval after my grandfather's early death in 1886. It was the interim period when O. B. and his brother C. H. Fuller leased the ranch from my widowed grandmother's manager. From that land they made a million dollars— when a million *was* a million. Their vast herds of cattle "mined" the wealth of nutrients straight out of the soil. Without sense of obligation to preserve the range, the Fullers never, in the early days, put back what had been taken. The over-grazing exterminated the gentle, nourishing perennial native bunch grass. Conservation of the land was not yet part of the cattleman's thinking.

As with human nature, even animal nature, waste had always been the keynote of plenty. In the case of wild animals, however, there were always periods of drought to set things right again. Under starving conditions the grass eaters were hunted down by hungry predators.

I still see O. B., an enormous genial man with a big paunch, riding a horse too small for him. His advice fit my father's determination not to replenish the range with tough Mediterranean grasses as the experts from the University of California at Davis advised. He repeatedly quoted O. B. whenever the subject came up: "Jimmy, let God Almighty feed your cattle!"

Faint sounds of the past drifted in on the air among the otherwise silent trees and made my roan sniff warily. The ranch buildings were gone. In our semi-arid climate there are ten-year cycles out of which nearly three years, marked by droughts, alternate more or less with three years of floods. The balance of years were often below normal rainfall. We were unprepared in our day for these hazards, not having the

money for underground water development and supplementary feeding. Nor could we afford to prevent erosion. Like the Spanish before us, with no recourse, we were continuously taken by surprise.

The Spanish had the reputation of being indolent and pleasure loving; the Indians as well. Fatalistic would have been a better word; it would have described the attitude we were forced to take. The balmy atmosphere between the extremes of weather that lulls the most wary also had something to do with our being unprepared. Caught too often by storms, these buildings were wiped out without a trace.

A decade, a natural unit of time, also cuts one off into forgetfulness. We were drawn into a curious attitude of *laissez faire*. My father's innate gentleness, which he inherited from his mother, as well as the lack of traditional agricultural know-how for this area may have been, on the other hand, the real factor. At any rate, except for the eucalyptus, the wild vegetation finally moved in to rub out all human signs of activity.

Nothing was left to justify the intrusion of these tall trees. Violent winds had chewed at their tops, denuding them of leaves, making them point rudely into the sky. In a flash I saw why the wild growth on the coast is characteristically soft and rounded, and fitted. Of course, the winds! But the quarrel with the indigenous vegetation was settled long ago.

Everything around this grove was swept clean, and bowed, and bent, and shaped, and molded; or carved to fit the contours. The wind was a master artist.

I rode down to the railroad tracks to the high fill put there by the Southern Pacific against my grandfather's wishes. It obstructed the view of the ocean. The loading corrals were made of massive timbers higher than a man on horseback. My father built them to outlast by far our family's ownership, though he had no intention of ever selling the land; nor is it likely that he ever intended to die. They were built as he was, a part of nature. Pepper trees were planted around them. Peppers are indigenous to Peru but like the eucalyptus (a transplant from Australia) they are more often thought of as native. Close up, they were ragged; a contrast to the willows that had feathered and neatly filled out in their broad space.

Recovery is characteristic of our California native vegetation. Natives left to themselves sooner or later always make a comeback when the rains arrive. They have been selected with the greatest care.

The big wind was gone. The quiet and peace were all the more effective because of the memory of it. I was recalling with nostalgia how in childhood we played games with the wind that was stiff enough to lean on. Then it was a happy laughing matter in spite of its wild disturbance.

The wind's absence brought peace to the mesas, allowing the earth's winter warmth to rise. "Growing weather," my father called it. Each time he carefully enunciated the words, and each time I could hear the grass growing.

The air was infinitely clear, and intensified the white light. I could not get enough of the flashing green world that day. I wanted to enjoy the silent peace. At any moment, without warning, the wind might return to blur everything. Attacking wildly, indiscriminately, it would violate that unbelievable silence.

The slight north wind I had encountered earlier stirred the silence by the corrals. It had not been strong enough to escape the funnelling canyons. It lazed through the peppers where the creek water finally slipped through the culvert under the tracks and emptied onto the beach. It came on and off; now only a little, then whispering, then stronger; at times, a little more purposeful. Relaxed, it still somehow insinuated a potential for violence—especially in its concentration against the great loading chute that dominated the complicated network of corrals below. The chute extended to the height of the fill where the railroad siding used to be.

Only days after my father's death, Southern Pacific railroad crews ripped up the siding tracks. The authorities apparently feared some descendant would discover that my grandfather had given to the railroad company over twenty miles of right-of-way, on condition that two loading sidings— two whistle stops—would be maintained by them in perpetuity. My father's life-long battle with the railroad, a Saint George and Dragon affair in the last century to ensure reimbursement for negligence that caused wildfires and death to cattle and horses as well as to keep open the claim before him, was suddenly, unceremoniously, and secretly reduced to an insignificant historical detail.

The first part of the hundred years was the last of the Spanish and Mexican era—the struggle with the elements. The second part was conservation, modernization, development. The third was liquidation and the transformation of the land

from family to luxury living. A beginning, a middle, and an end of an era.

My grandfather, the pioneer—a strong, determined man of action—was the one who could (and did) tell everyone to go to hell. After him came his youngest surviving son, my father, the gentle man who held it intact with his power of passivity, but with no less determination. Instead of losing one acre he added a thousand to what was left of his father's estate. He sat on his 39,000 acres like an old hen on a nest. Willing to work his way through droughts, disease and depressed markets, he made it.

His daughter, along with six of her generation who could not agree, had to keep it together until it could be sold for a fair price. Family dissension brought about the end of that era.

One massive gate in the old corrals creaked eerily in the slight wind. I was moved to dismount and look at the rusted "squeezers," which had been introduced in the last decade to avoid weight losses from the rough handling of cattle by ropers and the exorbitant waste of unskilled labor. Brand marks, burned into the fence posts to ensure distinguishable marks on the calves, will be the last to go. The scales, although rarely used, were still housed, and as before, quite sensitive to my slight weight. The corrals were as formidable as ever.

And the pitch down, they had reached it. Noise
    of wheels on stones, plashing of hooves in
    water; a world
Of sounds; no sight; the gentle thunder of water;
    the mare snorting, dipping her head, one
    knew,
    To look for footing, in the blackness, under the
    stream. The hushing and creaking of the
    sea-wind
In the passion of invisible willows.
               The mare stood still;
    the woman shouted to her; spared whip,
For a false leap would lose the track. . . .

Robinson Jeffers *Roan Stallion*

CHAPTER FOUR

The Beach

ON THE FOLLOWING DAY the first sign of dawn was a long, dull, silver band pulled over the ocean in the southeast. Then came a suggestion of red, low on the horizon, which quickly intensified into deeper red. From the barns on the hill where Old Roan was saddled, waiting for the early morning ride, the silver band changed into lead, revealing a broad stretch of low-lying clouds. Above the clouds an orange brightness developed, surrounded by an almost imperceptible pink. The gathering orange light gradually concentrated into a rich deep yellow where the sun was working its way out from behind the clouds. Colors constantly changed in those moments of watching from the colts' training corral. The wind blustered. A drilling barge was etched in black in the foreground of this vast expanse and in a strange off-centered way enhanced the composition. A helicopter's piston heartbeat far to the east was the only sound. The contraption, so far away, looked more like a dragonfly. Tiny, pinpointed, jet black, it blocked the low uncertain rays of light. Its intrusion was forgiven in the greatness of the morning light, for it was reduced to unimportance. Subdued like everything else in the sunrise, it took on the style of the place.

A forceful concentration of energy then gathered in the east. Described in terms of sound, it could have been a blast, except there was no sound even from the helicopter, which had come to rest on the drilling platform.

Breaking through like a blinding headlight, the sun reminded me of the orange passenger train lighting its way as it speeds by at night, scalloping precariously along the edge of the dark ocean. It turned the vast night sea into broad day. The heavy band of clouds resting on the horizon lightened, but small, dark, graceful strips within it still blocked the light. The band then turned into a soft pink-yellow haze that had the quality of daylight.

To my amazement there were no clouds after all. A broad path of light lay on the ocean surface from the horizon to the shore and was as blinding as the sun. The kelp line, caught in the path, was iridescent. The light was too much; I had to turn away.

Landward, light rays were only little by little catching hold of the greens and intensifying them. The black cast of morning made the greens glow. The night had not yet left them. The ubiquitous eucalyptus trees, pressing themselves to the front, were the first to catch the sparkles on their separate leaves, turning them into tiny reflecting mirrors. They achieved a conspicuous success only until the muted and more meaningful response of the native growth also rose to the sun.

As the greens moved into the light, a curious warmth pervaded the quiet air. The wind was stilled. The eerie feeling that was in the sunset two days before was now in the sunrise. In no time it was daylight, and the wind came back in an uncertain, cold, disturbing way, its character changed by the arrival of day.

Away from the sunrise and toward the hills, where the sagebrush and chaparral were laid on like a blanket, the black in the green held fast. The black of the soil in the plowed field below what we called the "Big House," which was our home, had its reflection in the hills. It gave a strange, powerful, earthbound quality to everything up there, everywhere to the north. The hills and the land below, pulling themselves up out of a deep sleep, were slow to accept the impatient sun. They reflected the deliberateness that is characteristic of this place—and of the people attached to it. It is a slow-moving, impervious coast. The geologists do not call it "old." The mesas were wave-cut benches 100,000 years ago, formed like our present terrace of rock ledges seen at the extreme low of minus tide. In the early dawn, that feeling of a prehistoric darkness dominated everything.

My father rarely left the ranch. Except for school, college, prospecting in Alaska, and some mining engineering in Mexico, he spent his whole life there. To help the other landowners he served two terms in Sacramento as State Senator, but he and my mother drove over eight hundred round trip miles every weekend to the ranches. He took loneliness for granted; it was his lifestyle. He actually sought it.

My mother was a complete contrast to my father. She was physically frail, her body hardly a support to her brilliant mind. She was tiny; even I, less than 5' 2", could look down on her. In her youth she weighed less than a hundred pounds. Her hair was golden and abundant, long enough to sit on.

My father never let her forget how beautiful it was. His admiration kept her from cutting it to suit the fashion. She had lively bright blue eyes and a typical Steffens face—not handsome but animated (my uncle "Steffie," Lincoln Steffens, her brother, was a journalist and author). She could laugh until she cried, and she talked at every opportunity. Her mind was a veritable bear trap. Too bad if you got caught in it! She was as intellectual as my father was not. She was strong as the strongest man when it came to defending her convictions.

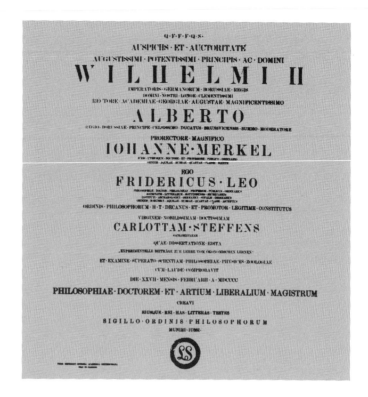

Coming from Sacramento and a city life, she was therefore not the ranch type, and never entered into ranch activities other than to apply her brilliant mind to its paperwork problems. Economics, politics, geology, background studies of all sorts were her interests. My father made no final decisions without consulting her.

Father's and mother's courtship was as unlikely as they were as a pair. They met in the pioneer class of Stanford University, and were engaged four years. During that time he prospected for gold in Alaska and she, without a word of German to start with, earned a Ph.D. in psychology in Göttingen, Germany. They were married in 1900. From then to the end of her 86 years she was only at the best of times a willing captive of the ranch; at others, she was more like a caged wild thing beating at the cage bars.

During his adult life my father never gave in to excesses or to behavior that could be criticized. He was a natural gentleman ("too handsome for a man," my mother said). He was always in good taste, as though on view. In 1956 when he sat by my mother's deathbed for a day and a night he did not once loosen his tie, nor did he lie down to rest. He sat stiffly in his chair—he was then eighty-five—for the length of the vigil.

In 1961, my father died suddenly. And he died as he had lived; after two days of a sudden and debilitating illness he rose from his pillow to brace himself on his elbows. "I'm done in," he said, and kissed me. I knew instinctively it was his good-bye. Later I saw the act as his last gesture of independence and an expression of his nineteenth-century gallantry. He was in charge of himself to the end.

My father's death revealed a clue to his life. When Lindbergh died, his wife Anne Morrow said: The great tree has fallen. You can at last see all of it. Once, on the ranch, I saw one of the giant live oaks toppled to the ground—these trees are old, old. This one had been down for some time, and in its present state I could see more clearly its enormous size. Trees that are standing never seem so large. There it was, slowly returning to the earth; its root system had been kicked into the air twice as high as a man's head. It had grandeur and greatness even in death, and it provided nourishment to all the life around it.

Footsteps on this land were rubbed out forever by his going. Those following would manage by phone or jeep or from city-based headquarters. For my father was not merely landlord, he was the exponent of our land, he was its product and its symbol. He was one of the last of the gentlemen cattlemen of the era of large family ranches in California.

For so much of my young life I took these two individuals—my parents—for granted as the sextant and star of our life there. They were its definition in the family context, their presence as much a reality in one sense as the other life, the wild one, dominated in the other.

Mounted on Old Roan and nearing the railroad tracks, I saw that the tide was high. The aggressive breakers pounded, muffled, on the soft sand. Sounds like rapid rifle fire erupted as each wave angled in an eastward direction along the south-facing shore down the coast.

A large hawk, too streamlined and purposeful to be the relaxed red-tailed hawk, scooted low over the tracks after the small fry that had not as yet made their way home to safety. The dark of night no longer protected them. A brown towhee lit on a Southern Pacific rail, becoming part of it as silhouette. Skittering along the rail, he turned this way and that, his long broad tail flapping wildly to stay his balance. He appeared to be in a surprisingly playful mood so early in the morning.

Across the tracks, black turnstones actually marked black and white, circled and swept over the breakers. Long-billed curlew stood upright in the foreground, silhouetted against the foam. The sun's rays low on the horizon blackened those wild shapes next to the swirling water. Above us a killdeer, running on the sand away from the sun, caught the soft light, which exposed him in detail. Starting and stopping in sudden movements, he appeared to be floating on a blur of pink legs.

Old Roan was dazed a bit by the enlarged waves flowing in and out under him. He tended to flow in and out with them. Had they not been rubbed out each time, his wandering tracks would have betrayed a rather heavy, drunken progress. He was mesmerized by the pull of the ocean. To avoid getting wet I had to direct him shoreward at each incoming wave. Given his head, he would have gone out of his depth. His distaste for the heavy, wet sand increased his predisposition to wander. A tug of war developed between us.

Long-billed curlew, killdeer and common snipe were busy at the water's edge. With too little dry sand on which to escape, they behaved in an uncharacteristic way. They were forced by the long waves to fly off in disorganized flocks. Heaps of seaweed—more than usual—cluttered the beach and contained debris from the oil platforms. It was a saddening sight, and it shocked me to a realization that a pure, wild beach would soon be no more. Yet, for the moment I was rich

beyond belief, dipping briefly, and perhaps for the last time, into this beautiful, doomed world. My morning ride was a lonely affair, to be treasured all to myself. Yet I felt a strange sense of guilt. Should I be so rewarded, even briefly? Should my luck perhaps not be shared? Might I somehow make of this sunrise something of a beginning, as it was meant to be, and not an end after all?

We continued on. The seawater, caught in depressions in the sand, bubbled as it sank. Everything was in a turmoil because of the plus tide, but in the churning, infinite riches of food were tossed up for the birds, wildly taking advantage of it.

In the distance a great blue heron stood with his feet in the water, characteristically facing out to sea, his near eye fastened on us. He posed: a silent, tidy counterbalance to the noise and feverish activity.

I felt the land was mine, and not entirely because I was a member of the family still its legal owners. I had somehow experienced the purity of the wilderness: I felt I had been in at its beginning and so could claim it as mine, in that sense. But at the same time I knew I was really only its steward. Yet what of the earlier eras when the Chumash bent the land a little to their needs? That certainly was a purer time. And before them, it was still more virgin. Probably I was only feeling my own beginning, my own earliest years connected with this particular environment. I was sensing the secret alliance of an individual spirit with nature.

Yet, I wondered why I felt so special. Any mortal could experience such an alliance no matter what his environment, if he made the effort.

The air on the beach had a summer quality, in spite of the dampness, and every cloud had mysteriously evaporated within the hour after sunrise. All the life, mostly birdlife— particularly the long-legged waders—were running and flapping as though there had been no night.

Homeward bound, with little time left, the roan and I found ourselves at the dilapidated granary in the midst of another extensive and ragged eucalyptus grove. The granary and the trees were pointing heartlessly to the end of our era; but the natives all around were unconcernedly still involved in the ten-year cycle, disregarding ownership, ambition, failures, or disappointments, feelings of loss. They will not quit these canyons until they are bulldozed out. Perhaps the hard seed laid down in the soil will from time to time send up new shoots to be pronounced as "nothing but weeds" until that supply, accumulated through the past decades, is also finally sealed off in cement.

Two eucalyptus branches touched. They made a rubbery, squeaking sound. A dow woodpecker, his head a vibrating red in the morning brightness, looked into a cavity in the dead eucalyptus—a hole that, by its appearance, he must have pecked out only the evening before. His recheck was brief.

Too soon it was late in the morning; I had to be on my way back. From the top of the hill on the east ridge of the home canyon, the sea was like opaque glass but all the more reflective. Light bounced off it, rippling and sparkling. Broad, pale

streaks paralleled the coastline; the kelp formed another
broad band that picked up the light. The surface appeared to
be impenetrable. An overall stillness descended—the usual
noontime doldrums. It was broken ever so slightly by a
breeze that blurred the illusion of glass. The sun then spread
over a third of the big ocean. It was too brilliant to look at
for more than a moment.

From the mesas, going home, I felt the potential grum-
blings of a hostile Pacific. (A push from the treacherous offshore winds can make the ocean boil.) Recalling the impassable chaparral high on the mountains, earlier in the year at
the San Augustine Canyon's end, and the white light, the in-
terminable blue skies, the soft air and the flaring greens of
winter, I anticipated a psychedelic explosion of color later in
the spring. After that there would be the rolling, golden-
brown hills of the in-between season, patterned by dark oaks,
black-green studded on gold, and finally, the overall tawny
brown of summer.

Every visit would be special; each time would be a new experience with an old friend.

If you would get exercise, go in search of the
springs of life . . .

Henry David Thoreau *The Natural History Essays*

CHAPTER FIVE

Month of the Beginning of Spring

THE COAST HAD CHANGED CHARACTER, or I was in a different mood. March, at any rate, was a disappointment after January when everything, because of too little rain, was in delicate balance. I had been anticipating the continuing tentativeness of the new growth that had been part of the heroic effort to carry on in spite of three preceding years of drought. There was also, earlier, January's characteristic will to live; on that trip I had seen that the subtle poignancy of deprivation need not mean defeat. It has a beauty of its own.

I had taken a step in my reeducation, but only to find this March a complete reversal. There was before me in every direction grossly over-grown vegetation—the rank aftermath of unexpected storms. Plants disciplined by the austerity of drought were overfed, fat. The scene came as a shock—my efforts to justify the hardships of January had to be adjusted to a different kind of understanding.

A bumper crop. Profit in the bank! It was not so easy to digest this total switch; and somehow the subject of money had lost its clout.

Driving to the ranch over punishing, hardbaked, rutted roads that dangerously shook the car might have prepared me for what was to come, if it had not been for the distraction of the fantastic beauty of the wild evening. On the last turn of the winding ranch road I was stopped by a blinding setting sun straight ahead. Without warning, it became a gigantic fireball, magnified beyond belief into a dark red, burning orb. Self-consciously, as though aware of its archaic and disturbing implications, the great ball settled itself neatly, perfectly, into a depression on the horizon. I watched, unbelieving, until it disappeared below the skyline. The old formula "Red sky at night, sailors' delight" raised my hopes for good weather. March in Southern California, according to the Chumash, is the "month of the beginning of spring" (*hesq momoy sqapuni*). But the violence of the scene should have been a tip-off.

Reaching into the mood of the place, I planned an early morning walk on the beach for the next day. The monotony of walking would be calming. I knew from past experience that it would help toward the big letdown I craved and that I associated with that country. I was long overdue for this because of the endless city demands that had pushed me into the attic of my consciousness. It was a need to unwind. To get back into my skin, perhaps. It meant literally even more a "going down" to meet the land where it lay, and to that level in myself where I had lived the determining years of my life. Our coast requires a descent always. For those new to the place the letdown is more often experienced as an unpleasant locked-in feeling, an immobilizing depression.

I had to find my place in the whole. I had to become an infinitesimal human replica of yesterday's sun cradled on the horizon. The settling-in would revive an old sensitiveness to natural things. An unstructured wandering on the beach would set things in motion: reflections, thoughts, little brain waves perhaps. On the elemental level, the greens would become greener, the wind would have a life of its own and animals would be on speaking terms. Inconspicuous wildflowers and forms would intensify and come out of their low-key camouflage that makes people pass them by. I already knew from experience that everything, eye to eye with nature, would subtly reveal itself. At these times the minutest scurrying things demonstrate the logistics of their perfect complicated structures. Their small lives become more significant in the intimacy of nature than those of big ones.

On the beach, finding shells turned into a minor but preoccupying game. Focusing helped me to forget. Seven hours of walking and wandering and looking did finally bring the welcome fatigue. I was in greater need than usual this trip because of the problems of liquidation. Big decisions had to be faced.

The one-foot, three-inch minus tide, a reminder of our moon's potency, made the beach surprisingly naked. Rocks, usually hidden, breached their slick waterworn surfaces. Innumerable tide pools came alive with the tiny clutter of scurrying hermit crabs—in cones and olives, mostly. Life was color-bright in the dark water. Young seaweed attached to the exposed rocks was a living green.

The naked rock ledges were disturbing; the unusual profile jarred me because of a need to relate to familiar routine feelings. I had little tolerance for distractions that day. The scene was not in keeping with the time of the year. Something formidable might be in the offing. Suspended flies bombarded like tiny soft pellets in the stillness, the swish of a mare's tail cloud in the north, an unexpected breeze from the west, high up, bothered me. Something was up.

By late afternoon, returning "home" to the superintendent's house, I started out to climb the San Augustine bank overlooking the beach to find the car. Not until then did the green of the pyramidal hill in the distance become suddenly, noticeably vivid against the rich dark blue haze of the mountains behind it. The hill had stepped up to be noticed. The oncoming evening, with slanting light filtering through it, turned the backdrop into a soft, dark, filmy substance.

The flies were now suspended shoulder high in huddles over the dry white sand against the bank. Caught in the sun they turned into minute, soft, mothlike things. Low sunrays had pinpointed and magnified the tiny obstacles. A concentrated stir among the plover indicated feeding time.

Summer tans were barely emerging. In the creases and swales, high up on the Bulito hill, far behind the barns, the mustard displayed its green-gold, rusted a little by burnt orange from poppies in the shale.

Sensibilities were at last on their way.

The house my mother had built on the ranch was her attempt
to reconcile, in her new wilderness home, who she was—her
city upbringing, her travels in Europe, university experiences
at Stanford and Göttingen (best of all was her amusement
when she discovered that rats in the attic had chewed up her
sheepskin Ph.D. diploma signed by the Kaiser himself). It
was a "town house," a grand affair for so isolated a place. It
had been designed by the best architect in San Francisco—although he had never been on the ranch. It had hardwood
floors and French doors and redwood panelling and gold cur-
tains. It was the rebellion she never articulated, for she always had to defend the ranch out of loyalty to my father. The
house had three stories, counting the attic. There was also a
cellar where we sat during the one or two hot spells each
summer. (Her Sacramento childhood had made her dread

heat.) A fine redwood stairway angled down (spiralling would have been too expensive) from the upstairs hallway into the living room, to remind her of the Governor's Mansion in Sacramento, originally her family's home.

Our shingled house was painted white. It shone in its isolation among the dark oaks towering over it, not blending at all with the wild country extending beyond mother's lush garden. It was more in keeping with the exotic trees and plants she had imported from foreign countries. It stood boldly out against the wild. It was certainly not the hacienda made fashionable by the Spaniards. It was "more likely the home of a local cattle baron," wrote a man named Chase whose book described the trails he travelled alone down the length of the coast of California many years ago.

Two great blue herons on the mesa east of the San Augustine Creek rose and flew away when they spied the car. Their message should have been clear. Shore-bound and distrustful, they always herald weather changes.

The preponderance of green turned the landward view into a landscape. In a painting, one could object to so much of one color, but a pervasive gentle mood offset my uneasiness.

A slight yellow tone in the green on the lower slopes was what was left of the mustard. It had been eaten down too early in the season by the Mexican cattle. Oaks had darkened to their summer green. Yin, associated here with winter, seemed to have expended herself; Yang still imperceptible, but quite ready to turn everything brown. I felt sad that the year's beginnings were over. The mystery had gone from the coast. Dark privacy was gone.

Nothing was left to be imagined; everything was there, immediate, overbearing. Flowers were full-blown; the foxtail, our summer scourge, had headed out. Soon there would be the harvest: fading of the flowers, a gradual death, and then seed. A summer's midday seemed to be taking over. Yang would soon be master, dethroning the lush green of winter's Yin. Still, something said: Don't be too sure.

I continued to note every detail, oblivious to their interpretations. By being thus compelled to note the most insignificant item as though it would otherwise be lost to the face of this earth, I was no different from the Taos Indians who must always greet the sun to help it rise.

Malva, now too tall, choked everything. Single blades of grass barely struggled through it. The alfilaria, a measure of good range, only a turf in January, stood tall and individualized. The pepper trees by the San Augustine corrals had not changed—that was to be expected.

The January silence had gone.

Lupine leaves and flowers bigger than ever remembered, the hard blue of their petals stood in a checkerboard contrast to the white. An orange poppy patch, in the shale beside the road, had become a smudge. Its petals were furled for the night. The tiny orange umbrellas were put away. Death and rebirth were united in the promise of seed. Erosion had been minor considering the all-time record rainfall. Here and there on the fields small rivulets flowing through the grass testified to the excess. In unlikely places water had churned violently.

Water gouged here and there across a few contours, yet a summer dryness permeated the air. Yin, dark, negative and feminine, was certainly giving over to her opposite number, positive, bright and masculine Yang. Something in the equation was wrong. Why should the creative principle not belong to lush winter in this country and why should Yin, associated with death (the vessel of renewal), not be the queen of scorching summer? It was certainly this way in the minds of those of us who worked the land and feared the six long, hot, dry summer months. Or are we more concerned with the feminine in our land? Or could we say that Yin becomes the creative, and Yang her opposite? (A surprising answer to this puzzle came by way of the Chumash. They also said in a story about their Sky People that the sun is the bringer of death. He is the man-eater.)

The barometer was still high but the wind continued to push out of the west. Instinctively, I tested it for storm possibilities. Facing into the wind I extended my right arm sideways as my father taught me years before. Fingers of my right hand once extended pointed due north where the storm could be. The west wind is often another sign of rain because northern storms move down the coast in wide circular sweeps. But the high barometer put me off.

The Gaviota peaks, brought into relief by the almost black hills at their feet, were faint and fair in the evening light. A feeling of green was in the black. Smooth "round bottom" hills extended along the coast. They cut sharply into the hazy background of the rugged mountains. The setting sun, its rays suddenly, sharply angled, lit the tops of the peaks. Many wild purple hyacinths grew along the banks of the road home. Their petals were no longer caught up in the tight knots. Overall, there was a subtropical mood. "El Rancho of

Heavenly Rest" my father's generation called it. Why should I be concerned?

Later, on reaching the small board and batten ranch house, I briefly noted clouds pushing angrily out of the west. Had I been more alert, I would have known without a doubt something was wrong.

What would the world be, once bereft
Of wet and of wilderness? Let them be left,
O let them be left, wildness and wet;
Long live the weeds and the wilderness yet.

Gerard Manley Hopkins *Inversnaid*

CHAPTER SIX

The Storm

A DELUGE DURING THE NIGHT made planning for the day useless. By morning two inches of rain had fallen; as the forecast had predicted, a two-inch sheet of water laid out on 39,000 acres. In the middle of the morning, over leisurely cups of coffee, I thought of my good luck the day before in escaping back to the ranch in mid-afternoon despite the prevailing dark and forbidding mood. I also relished revisioning the scene encountered on the way, especially the Mexican cattle gathered on the mesas in all their odd shapes and colors— many more than in the early morning. Some of them were milling in bunches on the road in continuous restless movements. Others seemed even more vigorous than in the morning: now grabbing at food on the trot, rudely pulling grass up by the roots and quickly, neatly, nibbling yellow mustard flowers. They were demonstrating what had happened to the yellow effect on the range that year. Individual animals taking their stand on the road held their own against me, making butting gestures at the car.

The last of the cattle from high back country over the home canyon poured down the precipitous fronting hills, hightailing it through the heavy sage, kicking, jumping, sliding. Like the others in the early morning they were wildly, dangerously playful. They were also moving to the mesas where the great blue herons had gone the day before in anticipation of rain. These birds always knew; they were truly reliable weather forecasters.

In the night, rain and wind slapped against the board and batten of the superintendent's little house. The eucalyptus over our heads whirled round in violent, erratic, mad dances. Distant breakers and still more distant thunder added to the confusion. Rain, wind and breakers combined their fury in a roaring turmoil throughout the night. There was some comfort in this pandemonium, for without a doubt it ensured a good year of plenty for beasts, plants, and man.

Listening to the storm gave me time to reminisce about our seacoast. The breakers, whatever their intensity, are indicators of the state of things. They also convey messages from distant lands—taking up the pressures from foreign storms thousands of miles away to spend them against our cliffs. The ocean limits the surrounding elements with its own mighty voice. So alive, it is like a faithful companion, a protector in the night. The power of the moon, too, had been reflected in the wide tidal swings.

That night, violence was only a variation on the theme— the ocean's other side. It comforted me in my snug hideout, promoting sleep.

The rain finally ceased by daybreak. But the minus tide would not turn from its extra high until late morning, so there was no use venturing out. The superintendent advised against a ride inland because the horse could never make it on the soaked trails. Reluctant to offer advice, he said in a near whisper: "Let the ground settle itself down a bit before riding to the beach." The ground had a life of its own? A familiar note—animism perhaps—but it seemed more like the natural feeling of a man intimate with the place.

Later in the day, being impatient, I had decided to go ahead on horseback and find out what he meant. The oozing ground, swollen and shifting in the saturating water, was treacherously undermined. Old Roan slipped and slid, his feet going in four directions at times. It was strange to see a horse so helpless. The old feelings of terra firma, the solid reliability taken for granted, all that one associates with the ground underfoot, were no more. There were no little islands of safety. That was my first conscious encounter with hostile land. It reminded me of bottomless bogs and quicksand experienced long ago in small estuaries formed by our larger creeks. I looked back with more awareness to the day our Indian pony sank to her belly, my brother and I hauling on the reins, forcing her to fight her way out. We were too young to fully grasp the horror of that predicament.

I could not remember having experienced a quarter of a mile like this—and it was all because I wanted a safe ride on the beach. The earth clung in masses to my shoes, sticking in heavy lumps of adobe we called "gumbo mud." I nearly gave up.

The ocean was not much more inviting. It churned and swirled and reared. Muddy runoff had turned it to a light dull brown. Mud still flowed from every stream, out of every culvert and indentation in the land. It streamed out of scalloped crests topping the banks as hundreds of tiny streams seeped down their fronts.

A broad continuous band of yellow foamed as breakers and swells piled up. There was not a square inch of quiet water anywhere; the tide had turned only because the tide book said it would. Nevertheless there was a thin telltale strip of raised sand, no longer reached by the waves. Storm pressures were still driving up the water.

In all this turmoil, the small snipe scuttled along the ebb of the surf, catching whatever was left exposed, hustling just out of reach of the incoming waves. A natural law was in control; they were tiny atoms of order within the unruly, law-breaking elements.

To the west the sky was a heavy gray with ominous black masses of clouds directly in the line of our progress. A cold and wettish wind came from that quarter like a spear thrust. Was a second storm brewing? Better not think about it. There was the blue sky to the south and east, which promoted wishful thinking for one bent on a long ride.

White cotton clouds hovered over the range, but they were rolled back on themselves by the wind. Down the coast, eastward and as far as the rounded green hills of the Alegría Canyon, the background was gray and almost blotted out. The perfect, almost rounded hilltops that always so pleased the senses now stood out sharply green against the gray.

Earlier storms had denuded the beach at the headlands. There was nothing but rock underfoot, and the deluge of the night before had scraped them clean. The exposed ledge, which extended from the high yellow earth banks until it dipped out of sight in the wild water, had a curious, chipped look, as though leveled off by chisel strokes. Centuries of wave action had done that.

Old Roan preferred the ledge to the sand dune, into which he tended to sink. He sniffed suspiciously at the smaller deposits in the rock. With frank disapproval he cleared them in wide, unexpected lunges. He spooked at the tiny earth slides from above and shied at every insignificant pebble rolling down the bank. He had a special distaste for the minute cave-ins on the small sandy banks of streams traversing the beach. His jumping and snorting finally got to me, infecting me with uneasy feelings and foreboding. The horse seemed particularly focused on something in the high, saturated cliffs. He continually pulled away from them. Landslides? Strangely he did not fuss at all at the piles of debris and mounds of kelp on the shining, slippery rock underfoot, nor did he mind the splashing waves.

Old Roan never stopped trying to double back for home and get out of the situation. He had more sense than I, who exerted all possible pressure to keep him moving forward. On hindsight, I am sure he was wary of the black horizon that should have been disturbing me.

Around the next headland, and past more rock ledges, we edged along a narrow pass against the bank where the waves were still smashing at the bits of white sand that were left there. Underfoot it was soft but not impassable; but Old Roan only snorted louder than ever.

Suddenly, the cold wind in our faces doubled in force, and with no warning clouds blacked out the sun and everything around us. Single fat raindrops fell in the bitter stinging cold; and then came the downpour. My mackintosh, which was made for fishing, not riding, only came to my knees. The horse slowed to a standstill in spite of my forcing. We endured for some minutes—then somehow the rain was no longer wet. It had turned into large hailstones that bounced off both of us.

Pandemonium hit the breakers. The streams of water flowing out of banks swelled to twice what they had been, new ones broke out everywhere and from places never before even associated with water. Breakers darkened into deep brown with the mud. The earth, rocks, water and mud broke loose as though there were no moorings left in the world. Over it all were the wild cries of shore birds. The drenching continued, intermittently relieved by hail. My shoes filled with water and my jeans were soaked from the knees down. The horse dripped water; his ears drooped dejectedly.

There was one alternative to our predicament: turn back and try to reach home. But I was not in my right mind; this was perhaps my last chance to face out a storm—to indulge in what few people ever feel anymore.

Horses in pasture back their rumps into a storm when it drives too hard; it is warmer that way. It was, and Old Roan calmed down a little. We hugged the bank to escape the whipping wind despite the eerie sense that something high up should not be trusted. Old Roan's suspicious behavior had undermined me—or possibly my own sensitivity was sharpening. Without the slightest warning a torrent broke out at our feet where it didn't belong. Old Roan recoiled and so did I. A long, wide, solid streak rushed across the clean gray sand into the yellow ocean foam. That kind of mud contamination of the ocean and beach confuses a lifelong sense of difference between sand and earth, in spite of their common origin.

We would have done better on the sheltered side of the next headland. Where we stood was too much in line with the gale, but to move at all was arduous. The horse seemed to agree with me; it was better to stay put, in spite of the beating.

The wait gave me time to register a mixture of feelings. There was first the foolish one for not having noted the black warnings in the west; but over and above that was the exhilaration that came from bearing out the crisis to its end. To be undefeated—so far—felt good. The sense of having endured in so wild a situation made me part of nature, part of all life. It was a chance to look out at nature from inside her. It was reassuring, too, to find once more that a bitter cold soaking does no real harm. I was able also to forget for a while the endless man-made devices in one's daily city life that are designed to prevent one from being fully alive. Overall was the need to experience the violence of the wild once more, perhaps for the last time, and, if possible, take at least some of it with me.

The drenching may have lasted half an hour and was followed, again with no warning, by a blazing hot, glaring sun. The shorebirds, particularly the killdeer and the willets, which had been screeching throughout the squall, were suddenly silenced. A solitary great blue heron still faced the direction of the storm, but this time with his neck pulled in. Snipe flew low over the foam. Many tiny beach flies stung me. The impact of their minute, solid bodies had the force of hailstones. They swarmed out of nowhere to be in the hot sun that was playing on the steaming banks.

From time to time black clouds gathered threateningly in the west, announced by alarmed cries of the birds. Now that

the storm had subsided, I could look around, and the wetting no longer mattered because of the heat.

Red-winged blackbirds were already dotting the sand. They were out of place, like the vultures I had seen once on the beach at La Paz. Their conspicuous markings and shrub-loving characteristics did not fit that setting. They were like people flocking to the beach on an unexpectedly sunny day in winter. The glistening green-black birds, with their startling red wing spots edged in yellow, sang ineffectually and incongruously against the breakers. Their songs were an odd contrast to the killdeer alarums—thin and shrill, synchronized and percussive. White gulls were flying low over my head in a slow, relaxed, orderly formation, enjoying the hot sun and the sudden quiet.

It was already past noon. In the east, great white clouds billowed in force. One dark rain cloud, apparently in the process of releasing some of its load, loomed up again in the west like a gigantic hand. The thick wrist rose on the horizon and the fingers reached into the clear blue sky. It was the mysterious signal to Elijah: *"Behold, there ariseth a little cloud out of the sea like unto a man's hand. The heaven was black with clouds and wind, and there was a great rain."* We were directly in its path yet still in the hot sun. The atmosphere was clear, the visibility nearly perfect. Like a magnet the clarity of the air drew close what was around us—the oil platform stood out clearly. Visibility also heralds a storm; yet what about the thorough scrubbing we had just had?

Beyond the San Augustine Canyon's cove, the headland had melted into a confusion of yellow earth—into shifts and slides loosened by the saturating water. One mass that had slipped was still leaning on the cliff face. Caves, cracks, and holes opened high up in the precarious jumble. Piles of earth were strewn over the sand. Old bench marks from ancient ocean levels on the cliff still barely showed. Much of the coastline had been chewed off and washed out to sea. All in all, as on land, it gave off a sense of impermanence and insecurity.

Old familiar sand dunes normally piled high against banks and cliffs were gone, leaving only small sand deposits here and there in crevices and corners out of reach of the onslaught of waves. The cement flume for the pipes laid out to sea for oil and gas was exposed, forming a barrier across the beach. Two days earlier it had been out of sight, submerged.

Flocks of godwits, their light brown color warm in the sun against the white and gray of the other birds, were maneuvering on the beach. The warm color tucked under their brown wings blazed into red when they flew. Cousins of the curlew, they stalked around like miniature storks with their necks pulled in.

We continued on up the beach in the direction of Point

Conception nearly as far as Little Cojo Cove. Large rocks stuck out of the sand and shallow water in a strange wild alignment. Old Roan once more sniffed and snorted and tried to turn back. His fear unnerved me. The minus tide, by now receded to its low ebb, left the tall, glistening black rocks boldly silhouetted. No longer just the remains of an ancient submerged rock stratum, they seemed to fulfill a mysterious purpose. Black shapes, strangely reminiscent of the eerie menhirs of Brittany, jutted from the flattened breakers. Ocean water churned white at their bases. The largest rock of all, a boulder, was set apart from the series. It barely surfaced, its bald top glistening. To this Old Roan said no, and he circled around it warily, snorting loudly. He would not be forced. For such a stable sensible horse, his fear and distrust of the rock surprised me. But I was sympathetic—it was indeed the head of a submerged monster.

Looking for giant limpets I dismounted and examined another rock in the shallow water. I had to reach the rock in the infrequent intervals between the biggest waves. Climbing up, holding the reins with my free hand, I caught several limpets before they clamped down with their forty-pound thrust. The knapsack for the shells somehow had to be kept from falling into the water. It was a balancing stunt on the slippery surface, made more so by thousands of tiny jets of water from sea anemones. There was always the danger of being washed off. The suspicious roan knew I was out of my head. His complaints were continuous. Each breaking wave sent him swinging round and round the rock. The deep water splashed over most of the rock and welled up to his cinch band. He could have reared, falling back on his reins, and broken free, leaving me to walk the seven miles home.

But by then we had both had enough. As we set out for home, relief showed in every movement of my horse. His ears pricked forward and there was a spring in his gait. His anticipation of home promised a long, peaceful journey for me. My only concern lay in the threat from the black cloud looming in the distance and moving toward us. The visibility again increased suddenly. Small details in the superstructure of the oil platform brightened. Out at sea, a freighter's bow and stern were visible. Its middle section appeared as though it were below the water, meaning the ship was beyond the horizon.

The rain cloud to the west came inexorably toward us, but, by some undeserved luck, it came only as far as the breaker line at our feet and then quickly veered back out to sea. It swung back and forth a second and a third time. Its abortive charges gave me, finally, some feeling of immunity. The willets refused to fly away unless we came right up to them. They seemed only mildly afraid of us. In flight they revealed striking black and white markings—broad black velvet appliqued to a background of white. The few times they left the sand they flew in long sweeps over the breakers and came in to land not far in front of us. They always kept to the same flight pattern. Finally, at the end of the cove, they doubled back and settled in peace behind us.

At three, and right on time, I heard the familiar relaxed jiggedy-jog of the orange-colored train, "The Daylight," as it slipped over the rail joints. When it came into sight without the usual fanfare and fuss, it looked caught by surprise. Its engine sounded a very long dragged-out "Ooo-oo" at each crossing. It chugged along languidly for a crack train; it seemed to belong there, and did not jar the feeling of the coast in the slightest. The noises it made recalled my childhood when we had no other way of telling time, and the sound of a whistle in the distance meant we were hopelessly late for lunch.

Puffy mounds of pure white foam, left by the outgoing tide, skidded slightly on the wet sand as we approached the home canyon. But behind us, our constant companion was the great black hand of rain, looming against the surrounding sky of clear bright blue. Its wrist still resting on the western horizon, the long, dark fingers of the hand now stretched directly overhead, angling across and far down the coast in the high wind. Out at sea, rain fell at intervals in dark, thick slanting streaks from the cloud's fingers.

The afternoon sun was low in the west, lighting up the

mist that rose from row upon row of churning breakers, like charging herds of phantom horses, their manes flowing in the wind. The mist had refracted the light in a way that intensified and magnified everything. The softening effect of the mist enhanced the brilliant green of the long, thin fringe of grass topping the cliffs and banks.

Over to the east, there were a few low-lying black and troubled clouds. The hand never left us. Overhead its fingers continued to stretch from out of the west and veer seaward. Far out to sea, a few clouds, lit by the sun, piled up gracefully like miniature castles and small towers. The shapes were delicate whirlwinds that pirouetted; otherwise, the sky was cloudless. Dark green seaweed showed in the minus tide, and streamers of green brightened the brown kelp. The sparkling foam bubbled and popped on the sand as the sun lowered almost to the sea's horizon. The foam scudded a bit in the slight wind; some of it slid out on the tide. In it were yellow and pink and green lights that shone like diamonds.

By five o'clock it was quiet enough to hear the small birds in the brush on the low banks. Only the breakers stirred. All else was serene in the long shadows. The horizontal evening light brought out the white of the churning water, making it glow in the mist that was blown out to sea from the turmoil.

Big shorebirds were very much in evidence. Walking as though performing a stately dance, they jutted their necks out and back like East Indian dancers. Among them were round-bodied black turnstones, black and white with long black vests. The little snipe, shining white and no longer so drab as they had appeared in the stormy overcast, were busy pecking their supper.

Creeks tumbled out of the large culverts under the track's right-of-way. By then I was walking to get the stiffness out of my bones, so in order to cross and stay dry I had to remount Old Roan each time we came to a stream. My saddle was weighted down with a sack of abalone shells, and my knapsack had to be treated gently, because it was full of frail shells. With my stiffness, mounting became a chore. After the first sprightly move toward home, Old Roan resumed his jumping each time a pebble rolled down the cliff. He grunted at the few tiny mudballs and cave-ins made by the streams rushing across the sand to meet the incoming tide. At each crossing he lowered his muzzle, sniffed at the water, groaned and sighed miserably. But as yet, no complaints about the ocean. Apparently he was not going to forgive me for the morning's huddle against the cliff.

One last look to the west in the path of the setting sun revealed miles of churning breakers, their mist and foam lifted high. It was a lovely vista, tender and luminous, and infinite. The broad band of moving white water along the breaker line swept gracefully with the curve of the coast. It extended all the way to the sun, which now rested on the water. Breaker beyond breaker beyond breaker were topped, softened and lighted.

We were ushered around the last headland by the few remaining rays of the sun not yet lost to the sea's depths. They were exactly at the point of being cut off by the horizon, but in the last moment the rays lit the small, smooth pebbles scattered over the wet sand, making each one a tiny lantern in the black. The shore was carpeted with softly glowing lights, like those of fireflies.

It was dark on land when we climbed up at the home canyon. The big clouds behind the sentinel hills of the Bulito were a mysterious smoke color. They were massed and softened at first sight, and rounded. In no time, they took on something of the seashells below them, more salmon than pink.

It was hard to let go of the sight in order to open the stiff gate at the tracks, but I had to hurry because black night was about to descend. Twilight is very brief at this latitude.

A last look at the sea was barely possible but essential. The familiar abalone colors had surfaced and the sea had calmed. It was as though it were content at last to be put to bed by night.

The drama that was there that day was something to talk about; yet, paradoxically, there was a stronger need to be silent. It was too personal a matter to discuss, and the others sensed this when I reached the house. The superintendent merely said, "We thought about you during the cloudburst." No questions were asked. They somehow knew the experience on the beach was part of a personal farewell to the land of my beginning.

The tides are in our veins, we still mirror the stars,
life is your child, but there is in me
Older and harder than life and more impartial,
    the eye
that watched before there was an ocean.

Robinson Jeffers *Continent's End*

CHAPTER SEVEN

Across the Mesas and Down the Cojo Canyon

OLD ROAN WAS SADDLED, waiting and ready to go. Although tied to the superintendent's truck in front of the house, he could not be seen because it was still dark. It was his snuffling that caught my attention. Immediately, I was reminded of an exchange with Tom at the corrals. I told him I planned a long ride. "You like your own company, don't you?" he said. I thought no more about it and was prepared to get Old Roan myself that early Sunday morning. Besides, it was rest time for the men who had worked so hard. But there, in the predawn, Old Roan was swinging on his rope, eager to move out.

It was a beautiful, warm, clear day as I started overland across the mesas. The tide was too high for the beach. My plan was to ride into the Barranco Hondo ("deep gorge") Canyon and cut over to the west, across the ridges where the Barranco Hondo, Gato, Cementerio and Cojo canyons come together at their common source. This highest spot on our mountain range we called "the lookout" and was originally named *Tepitates*. (Kote Lutah, a leader of the small surviving band of Chumash, told me it meant "a sacred high place.") From the jeep road leading to the lookout I could drop into the Cojo Canyon and down to the beach where the heavy wooden gate at the railroad crossing could be pushed open, at least to a "V" wide enough for Old Roan to squirm his way through.

One gray conical hill ahead of us just west of our barns was topped by a green-yellow crown of mustard. It seemed to be deliberately mocking one of our varieties of small sparrows—nondescript, but sporting an incongruous green-yellow cap.

An import from foreign lands, the young mustard in its abundance seemed intent on driving us off the coast. It had in fact already reduced our best range drastically below the profit line. In some areas the broad-leaved malva commandeered most of what was left of the bare places. One could determine there were also grasses and clovers only by noticing the Mexican cattle, their muzzles down and out of sight in the growth.

My grandfather enjoyed the grandstand; he was gregarious and entrepreneurial—his farsightedness, money, and ambition helped launch the Southern Pacific Railroad. It didn't become operable, however, until after he died. The railroad commandeers sixty feet of right-of-way along the coast, donated by my grandfather as his part in the promotion. It extends along the twenty-mile stretch that crossed our land.

My parents were the first passengers on the Southern Pacific line. Father brought his bride to the ranch in the caboose of the train my grandfather had helped put through. It was the train crew's car. We had no roads or phones or means of travel other than by railroad, horseback, or foot. In exchange for right-of-way along the coast, two whistle stops were made available to us to use for passengers and shipping cattle. The train lacked the ordinary luxuries of the times—it could also be as much as a half-day late, forcing us to wait on the siding for the moment when, without warning, it would suddenly appear. The only advance signal was from a semaphore nearby. Because of the rough terrain, the engine could not be seen until it was practically on top of us. To stop it, someone had to wave a flag until the engineer tooted twice in recognition, and with creaking and clanking and streams of steam, brought his monster to a halt for us to board.

I felt the silence pressing in on my skin from all sides. Heavy as the silence was, it was broken slightly by the small bell-like sounds of startled birds and by the distant ocean breakers. I realized with pleasure that these very sounds were responsible for the impact of the silence. A western meadowlark sang without interference in all that quiet and space. His call-song was a golden declaration of territorial rights; it was at first close by, then farther away, and again and again, still farther away. His openly announced retreat was orderly. In his own way he added to the stillness. How characteristic of nature to warn away an unwanted newcomer with a weapon of song. Aesthetics were subordinated to the needs of survival and in their function had become even more beautiful. Beside the road there was a giant malva, at least twelve inches high, its broad, flat, dark green leaves forming a small canopy. It flourished comfortably by itself.

The morning was typical of California, a land reveling in color, softened and blended in the early morning sunshine and stillness. A dull, gray fog reached down over the back range like someone trying to climb over a wall.

Finally, at the San Augustine Canyon, there were two small pyramidal hills painted orange with poppies. Other smaller ones behind them were covered with delicate mustard blooms stirring slightly on tall thin stalks. By then the fog on the ridge had given up and backed down nearly out of sight. Over the channel, small mare's tail clouds drifted in an uncertain sky. A persistent meadowlark nearby gave us his liquid, throaty melody. Green-black oaks made a pattern against the white shale.

The blue extravaganza on the rolling mesa at the San Augustine Canyon was lupine. It stopped me. Never mind the many miles yet to ride. Looking, I tried to make some of it mine but failed—unless that recognizing it as a piece of heaven on earth was enough.

The color, which was laid out across the mesas and softened in the light, was neither masculine nor feminine. The blue was not quite powder blue, the yellow had depth, the deep orange had become a burned-out red and the grass bursting out of the ground here and there was a rank, rough blue-green. The meadowlarks did not overdo it, but one red-winged blackbird did; he dominated with his thin, high-pitched screech. But his shining black body with its gaudy brilliant red spot rimmed in yellow was lost against the mustard flowers. The alfilaria—or "fillaree" as we called it—was thick with microscopic, dull lavender flowers and clusters of pods like tiny green storks' bills rigidly pointing skyward. A horned lark, not much bigger than a sparrow, his feathered horns standing out in clear black velvet, caught my eye as he fed determinedly on the ground among small plants. The Chumash knew what they were about when they called April *neg momay an capipquees* ("month when the flowers are already in bloom").

Just beyond the San Augustine, across the creek and high up, poppies in the Llegua Canyon nestled into the green and yellow. The poppies close by were sunlit, their petals still open in the warm, early rays. A distant mourning dove added a soft, saddened note, incongruous in a creature so heartless. The cicada sang on regardless of us. In the area of the Llegua and Barranco Hondo mesas, still farther west, a sea lion surfaced in the breakers. His watery bark, magnified by the expanse of ocean, was curiously fitting.

The mesas, in contrast to the overgrown hill cover, were as though mowed, which is characteristic of dryland pasture planted there—our attempt to shorten the long dry summer gap for our cattle. To the north, a pinch of brighter yellow shone between two hills, outlined in a graceful curve of shale strata high up. Black oaks, in contrast, whitened the shale and intensified a thin sprinkling of yellow poppies. In the dust by the roan's front hoof, as we stopped to enjoy the color, I saw an unusually large glistening stink bug with his rear stuck up for trouble. Nothing was too small to notice. I pulled the roan away so he would not step on him. The Chumash story of Coyote, foiled by a stink bug in his attempt to drink in the land of the spirits, came to mind. In this legend the bug had stretched himself enough to cover the pool. Aboriginal respect for the power of insects always intrigued me.

The mesas were exuberantly strewn with flowers all the way to the gate, into the area of steep hillsides covered with sage.

The first task that day was to note the flowers in detail: the tiny yellow sour clover, the soft brownish clusters with whitish scallops on their leaves—the Spanish clover; the sunflowers with their wild, sweet, tantalizing scent that differs from the musty sweetness of mustard blooms. Tidytips everywhere; tiny with broad white scallops and centers of yellow dotted with minute brown spots, their scent may be beyond human detection. California poppies were wide open in the

Barranco Hondo Canyon, where they are protected. Giant red paintbrushes, subtly different in color from the poppies, were abundant.

Even in color there was nature's will to be different—to avoid repetition. The rough blue lupine had a cooling effect. A small flower the color of goldenrod bears the curious name "goldfields." There were also the bloodless yellow of the elderberry trees, the mottled pink of the sweet peas and the white chickweed flowers, blooming by the thousands on their small plants.

The wild oats were heading out. Here and there giant thistles, called milk thistles, imports from the Mediterranean, were aggressive in their promise of great royal purple heads. In the summertime, the spines must be managed gingerly; our horses mouthed the mature heads for their seeds. Lupine fingers were relaxed and opened. Superb morning glories showed off their mauve stays. Here, paintbrushes like raspberry sherbet made a necessary, harsh countereffect to the almost too-perfect scene.

Past the gate a large oak stood shrouded in new leaves and the long brown tassels of early spring. The fresh green of the oak was swallowed up by the abundant mature green around it. Beyond was an "all's well" watchman call of the quail—a single note that rang out reassuringly. The paterfamilias, with his black velvet bib lined in white and his forward-looking plume, was perched on the sage, vigilant. (I am told he takes his turn on the nest, but I have never seen a hen on guard in the wild.)

In order to stretch my legs a bit, I walked to the gate. The heavy grass and weed cover stropped my shoes, giving them a shine. Old Roan slipped and slid. Underfoot, the vegetation was slippery as ice. The superintendent had told me that morning to stick to the worn trails. It was not hard to see why.

A flutter of wings, a fuss and low warning sounds: our quail had plummeted to the ground from his lookout and could be heard talking over the situation. We were too close. Soon all was pointedly silent. Undoubtedly, there were tiny puff-ball young somewhere about, camouflaged by dark stripes, so little they could only freeze and wait for the danger to pass. Yet sometimes they allowed themselves to be squashed underfoot rather than move.

No riders of the purple sage in this God's country. It was too intimate for that. Creek water, ordinarily furtive, was frankly flowing. Energy and substance ran clear, clean and full down its ancient course to the sea.

House finches were everywhere; somehow, they seemed wrong away from houses. A dead branch jutted out over the tops of a green oak emerging from a rotten stump. It pointed upward with a slight, insinuating lefthand twist from where it had broken off, like a great black serpent surveying the area. Two nights before I had had a dream; such a snake had left its hole and had to be driven back by some mechanical contraption. The serpent in the Garden of Eden. "Trouble in paradise," one of our advisers said when he was told about our family conflicts.

There was a sound like thunder, and a white vapor streak shot up behind the ridge, high up and out to sea, then abruptly ended. Old Roan cringed, his legs seeming to bend under him. No snorts or jumps this time. It was a missile from Vandenberg Field. It faded out of sight over the ocean, the sun no longer in line to pick up its vapor trail. Old Roan shook for a long time.

When the shock was over and Old Roan calmed down, I noted how the sage was alive with bees, buzzing flies, all kinds of insects. Among the insects was a tiny russet hummingbird in continuous flight shining in the sun. His thin, shrill, tiny voice pierced the air. More birds—varieties of sparrows, juncos, jays—came forward but disregarded us. The quail were also muffled now and whickering deep in the brush. They added to the general sense of coming-to-life. Unidentifiable sounds struck up as normal routines were resumed. As always the morning glory flaunted its small victories over acres of heavily massed sage.

Some sage in the canyon was white. White hyacinths grew scattered through it, as well as along the jeep road. The *trrrt trrrt* of a downy woodpecker pierced the quiet of an oak grove across the creek. His quick short runs along a rotten stump and the bob of his head as he circled were easy to picture. At the crossing the creek water had spread onto the road, making a bog; large rocks jutted menacingly out of the deep mud. Old Roan stepped gingerly into this mass, his hooves slipping and sinking among the rocks. His body careened, corkscrewed and undulated, becoming a dubiously safe perch. His loud snorts stirred small spasms of fear in me. His little self-tortures invariably infected me when we were alone and so far away, and he knew it. Picking his way through the rounded rocks he seemed to float with no legs at all. Such tentativeness made me doubt that four legs are an improvement over two.

A few shriveled red berries on an old toyon bush reminded me of Christmas. The sage gentled the hillside to the softness of wool. Where the canyon opened, salt cakes were white against the green grass and yellow mustard. One was at a rakish angle, its corners licked off.

The back country was still dangerously wet. A massive feeding bin had been knocked over by the wind; it was hard to believe the wind could have been that strong.

Beyond the rock ledges that extend the length of the coast, the oaks joined the anonymity of sounds and scents. The silence was not accidental. We were expected. A secret, private time for nesting—a time of balance. Light, leaf, shade and modest flower, and the briefest glimpses of the birds were part of it. I thought again of nature's timing: how nests were in the making when vegetation was at its fullest and could provide protective screening.

Clearly there was busy and vast preparation for the production of new life. The birds must rush to build their precarious little homes and hurriedly raise their frighteningly helpless young to a point of independence before the intervention of some awful calamity: an army of predators equally in need and waiting. "All or nothing" in a bird's life; and what luck when a youngster is seen, still showing the clownish tuft of down on its head, clumsily following after its harassed father.

Above the ledge, nature's fantastic screening was at its best. Signs of life in the trees became unexpected gifts. Rustling sounds referred to what was going on. The Chinese have a word for it: Tao ("The Way"). Everything in its right place, creation and destruction in balance. The hummingbird sage with sticky red flower clusters in the dark oak shade was crudely fitting.

The noise of insects in the still, heavy air rose above the running stream. The yellow of the new oak leaves meshed with the distant mustard glimpsed through the tree canopy high on the ridge. The urgency of courtship steadily mounted in the birds' songs—but always out of sight. Abundance, creating a sense of exuberance, was the stimulus; food was not a problem.

Light filtered from all sides into a clearing in the oaks silkened by delicate green grass and a scattering of white hyacinths. These oaks higher up were particularly battered and bent; they had been stunted, and great age showed in the twisting and gnarling of their rotting limbs. New green leaves and the profusion of surrounding shrubs saved them from casting gloom. An Anna's hummingbird buzzed its wings close to my ear, and a great horned owl sped on nearly fixed wings through the dense foliage like a giant gray moth. He added a nighttime feeling to the bright midday.

A brilliant red star-shaped flower, flaring out at the end of a long brown neck, grew out of a crack in a boulder at the second ledge. There was orange in the red, possibly from the sun. Fluffy lavender flowers, a little like deadly nightshade but lacking its ominous quality and its daggerlike centers, were springing underfoot.

Large oak limbs lay in the trail, causing firmly established detours well-worn by cattle and wildlife. Prickly phlox and sweet peas added to the surprising number of lavender flowers everywhere. It was necessary to lead Old Roan over a boulder to avoid a narrow place. He jumped onto it like a goat. I wondered how he knew the sandstone rock surface was soft enough for his hooves to dig in.

Our high-shouldered Mexican cattle, camouflaged by the spotty shade of the small oak grove high on the ridge, surveyed us curiously. They were like the other cattle in shape and color and as always looked with astonished eyes over the brush at us. We climbed laboriously toward them, Old Roan pouring sweat, his saddle slipping, to where they had bedded down in the night. Great nests were flattened into the tall grass. It was cozy there out of the wind and with a view that was enormous: the whole coastline lay before us as far as I could see, and ridges, one beyond the other, stretched out of sight, as in an ancient Chinese silk painting.

Past noon I had to close my eyes against the glaring green. Shining waxy-rich buttercups were plentiful in the grass; other flowers were soft round yellow buttons. Yellow predominated in the sun; purple seemed to flourish in the shade.

The last steep stretch took us past the *chilicote*, or man root. This one had fruit—some of it lay on the ground, half eaten by the cattle.

Between the Barranco Hondo and the Cojo, looking up and to the north, were great soft sandstone ledges leaning over us. They were part of our northern boundary. The wind had carved odd shapes in the boulders. Spreading great wings in the hot sun, buzzards preened themselves there. One had to look closely to separate them from the sandstone. This is where the Santa Ynez range dwindles out to the sea. (I did not know it then, but I was looking at my future home site.) A cool welcome sea breeze funnelled up the Cojo from Point Conception.

At the top, the lookout was in bloom: flowering chaparral, indian warriors, yellow twining snapdragons, golden-topped grass (an import), blue-eyed grass, iris, wild sweet pea, alpine shooting stars, fiesta flowers and many giant red paintbrushes.

In a protective swale at the head of the Cojo, varieties of paintbrush flourished. They specialized in reds, from the palest tints verging on pink to the reddest hue. But in all these shades there remained a reminiscence of pink. It was hard to imagine ordinary red with pink in it but there it was. The colors were intensified by the overhead mist heavy with rain. The first ceanothus (deer brush) we encountered in the canyon was pale blue, almost white, a color never found in the nurseries. Possibly it is too frail to stand domestication.

Old Roan refused to negotiate a deep bog on the old jeep

road. As we dropped down, he reared back dangerously when I pushed him. He must have known it was the overflow of a permanent spring. Below the bog it was also impassable. Finally, we had to climb above it through heavy brush, taking a miserable, wide detour that cost us valuable time and energy. That bog is a year-round problem.

The Cojo Canyon looked as though it had been mowed. Now that the cattle had moved on, the lawn effect of that rough terrain was surprising. I wondered about the methodical ways of the cattle.

From the detour the creek sounds increased. We came on another ceanothus, this one darker blue. Looking at it closely, the color was in millions of microscopic, deep blue centers to clusters of flowers that were almost white. The scent was surprisingly sweet; if it could have been eaten, it would have had a gamy taste. A young pepperwood tree grew out of the bank, far away from its San Augustine home. Unlike the others, it was doing well. I had never before seen a volunteer pepper.

Tall trees in the creek below were topped by wide leafy flat-green hats—uncompromisingly flat hats that only a very smart woman would dare to wear. But absurdly flowing beards of delicate pink streamed from under the flat hats to spoil the metaphor. It was early spring growth. Above, the high ledge by the lookout road had become subdued in the luxuriant growth; it had lost the forbidding bareness of three years of drought.

The elusive scents seemed associated with the unknown part of human nature, perhaps the deepest part. It is something I like to think we share with wildlife. At any rate, I was content to let much of it escape me to take up again another day. It was not the time to try to be conclusive. Other confrontations at other times would revive the issue. Besides, scents and smells would always be a tie to my unknown side. The bulk of my life had been lived through my eyes and ears and touch, not my nose.

The lupine, the small yellow flowers, the California poppies and the pale transparent sticky monkeyflowers (the color of bone) had no scent at all. Of the others, there was the contrasting sweetness of the ceanothus, the shasta or oxeye daisy, the bush sunflower and the sage, and the elusive, heavy and pungent mustard that comes in on the wind. The sage smell has the most character. But the pittisporum at the "Big House" is so heavily perfumed that it almost carries you away. Untamed scents differ from the tamed in the way a tribesman differs from his city cousin. Life is mostly divided into two worlds: the one that is outwardly free and clear, within nature's limitless boundaries, remains controlled by an inner natural territorial law; the other, cultivated in a broader sense within its individuality and pushed away from nature, manipulates and adapts, outwardly, according to ego needs.

The Cojo hills are not part of the Santa Ynez range because the Cojo Canyon veers off in a westerly direction. Because the Cojo is not in line with the prevailing north wind, it was quiet and flaunted poppy patches and yellow mustard where the soil was deep. There were fewer oaks than in the Barranco Hondo. Many had keeled over and lay prostrate, but enough roots remained intact to keep the trees alive. Their root systems were too shallow to stand the long succession of dry years, and they gave way when heavy rains softened the ground. Several huge oaks had fallen, spanning the creek like bridges; sad to see the ancient ones laid low. None will ever be replaced. Cattle and deer relish the tender seedlings too much.

Fresh badger holes, dangerous to horses, menaced the open spaces.

There were signs of bigger-than-usual life, part of nature's underworld. The possibility of sighting the two albino coyotes seen there recently by the superintendent made the lower part of the Cojo more special.

Being on the alert for these creatures (apparently still not ready to show themselves) sent me back to our childhood dreams. Like the Indians before us, all our years on the ranch we strained to catch sight of these creatures. A white coyote or a white deer carried a special message. How universal a symbol this was, from the beginning of time on, we couldn't have known when we were children—or why. We had no way of knowing, for instance, about Crazy Horse of the Oglala Sioux. As a young man he saw a white buffalo and knew then he was destined to lead his people in their last fight for freedom. And that day, had the pair of albinos in the Cojo deigned to appear I could not, would not have asked for more.

Later at the beach, the giant limpets I saw in March were clustered on the rocks, entirely exposed. The lack of wind left the tidewaters within the natural pull of the moon. I found the ocean dull; more than likely I was tired. Seven hours riding, and the resultant stiffness, were gaining on me. Old Roan, "green" and fat because of his luxuriant pasture, was drenched in sweat. (He was a "good keeper," as those animals who efficiently metabolize their feed are called, but in the end it was his undoing.) Stumbling unnecessarily, his hind leg periodically sagging, he laboriously made his way on the sand. Possibly his feet were tender, but more likely he was tired, like me. He never stopped reminding me of his overall distaste for this peripatetic folly of mine. Led, he dragged back on his reins. I was annoyed. A big baby, and *I* should carry *him* now!

The beach birds appeared to be in mourning, except for a small killdeer-type of bird; they were numerous and quite oblivious of us. Another small bird with a black head and black and white wings may have been a juvenile or was in courting plumage. Most of the birds with black backs wore deep black vests. One bird was solid black except for a white underside that showed a little when he ran. In flight he was a balance of dark and light.

A faint whinny came on the air as we neared home. Old Roan stopped and threw up his head in a loud lonesome answer. If homesickness had been his trouble, he should have been more eager to move.

The sky was as gray as the water and the water as gray as the sand.

O how can it be that the ground
                does not sicken?
How can you be alive, you
                growths of spring?

Walt Whitman *This Compost*

CHAPTER EIGHT

The Alegría Canyon

OCTOBER AND NOVEMBER, the year's nadir, is normally the dead time of year. The unexpected rain that had occurred a month too early was confusing things. In spite of the dominant gray, small fine green grass cropped up in spots like punctuation in a paragraph.

The Alegría, with its whispering secrecy and quiet, reminded me of a great sleeping animal that appears to be dead, though the slow, relaxed rise and fall of its breathing reveals otherwise. So it was with the canyon resting, waiting hopefully, if not apprehensively, for more rain. Should the rains come on time, there would be cause for exuberance; should they not, stolid acceptance. There was much to read in that one small glimpse into the lower reaches of the Alegría.

In a vast untouched area like ours, you can hear what you need to hear. You can see for your own good. Messages come through your touch. You are soaked, submerged, immersed; full to the brim with beauty. Each visit can be a final answer, but the next visit brings you something else. It never ends. It becomes an endless process: you and nature have become one and you borrow its infinitude. You then have to go back again and again, because each time you outgrow, in some way, the self you were before.

You struggle for the words to make nature finite, to capture her, to take her with you, and you are defeated, which is right.

The day before from Tepitates I had seen a thick layer of fog roll shoreward across the channel. It extended all the way to the island bases, making them appear to be resting on clouds. This did not relieve the worry about drought, nor did another sign of rain, a view of the islands so clear that their canyons and ridges were visible. From years of experience I knew that at the last moment the most favorable conditions could be a letdown. Promise is characteristic of drought. A number of brief signs of rain and their disappearance at the start of the season are sure signs of a punishing dry year. Nature's will to create is gone—or, from nature's perspective, a rest period for the land is indicated, and then a fresh start.

I felt the impersonal quality of the cold, which matched the graying mustard. Death of the year—any year—is so utterly impersonal. By contrast then, is life personal?

In the fall the land is a composition of earth colors—subtle, hardly noticeable browns, hennas and oranges. Ground colors, with so much vegetation gone, were having their brief day. Life had gone to earth, had gone underground. Energy and life were lost to view.

Sounds and scents, just as fleeting as the colors, were also faint; the scent was an essence, as the sounding wind was a presence. But it is the sound of silence that carries one away.

Will Big Coyote of the Chumash win the game of chance and bring us plenty, or will Sun and Eagle parch us?

Yet the uniqueness of the coast here directly relates to the lack of rainfall. Its overwhelming attraction is as much, if not more, the outcome of harsh conditions as of benevolent rains. Droughts have always been with us—three years out of ten, and at least one exaggeratedly dry. The twisted, gnarled oaks, the snarled shrubbery, the tough sage with its delicate tentative lavender and white flowers in perverse ways prove the beneficence of dry years. Life, desperately but surely hanging on until the next rain—no matter how slight—gives the place an overall sense of beauty in strength. The desert cactus, a miracle of even greater tenaciousness, helps to make the Southwest what it is.

Unfortunately, in the cattle business long dormant periods mean bankruptcy; and there is no comeback. But nature's life force returns. The hard seed lying in the ground, no matter how long, sprouts and sets into motion the food chain.

The essence of the land, as it has been since the beginning of time—its evolution—still needs to be translated for human understanding. Descriptions, impacts, impressions come from the human side; but what is nature's view of us humans? What would the message be if a tree spoke to us, or an animal, or an insect? What would come from "out there"? Would "the other" in nature reach into "the other" in ourselves? If only it would.

So many thoughts, and for whom? The world is drowned by thoughts, most of them watered-down to satisfy too many people. But there is the need to capture the real stuff of this coast, no matter how difficult and personal and elusive a task it is. My notes need no justification; they are a thing in themselves, just as the coast is. Besides, one needs to have a say in one's old age.

As I walked along the beach later that day, a motor fishing boat paralleled along the shore, with its powerful, encroaching, self-assured engine noises. It was barely outside the breakers. To shut it out of my consciousness I carefully noted in detail what was around me. So that was it. Even though often redundant, my notes were also my protection.

In the afternoon the ocean began to build for the incoming tide, and the gray overcast mounted heavily out of the west. It moved deliberately toward the south where storms gather for the final push. Dampness in the air gave off the sense of a storm already spent; yet, underfoot, it was still crisply dry. There was not a sign of life at the beach.

I wanted to hurry home. I was a little frightened, yet there was absolutely nothing to fear. I had an unaccountable feeling of crisis that comes with the uneasy dusk as it also does with the dawn. Since it is neither day nor night it is a strange time. And it never lasts long enough for one to become used to it.

Standing there, watching, color finally came to the clouds, promising a vivid sunset. I knew it would be a brief one; there would be a flash of color, then the dark.

In the foreground there was no differentiation between sand and sea. The light shafts, at first so faint, were becoming distinct. There had to be open skies somewhere, for the sea kicked up a very bright sparkle in places. Wide, soft light bands intensified and searched downward. Three islands—San Miguel, Santa Rosa, and Santa Cruz—displayed their ridge tops in the descending sun; they stood out above the general faintness around their island bases.

I had a driving need to prove the uniqueness of this country. My fate was deeply involved in it.

Abalone shades of pearl, gray and pink drifted into the distant clouds. The sun, descending more and more, suddenly lightened the sky to the west, forcing into the northeast a contrasting heaviness. Rays from the sun, now on the western horizon, pointed up a white swish of vapor above, cutting through the layers of gray. Minutes later sun rays shot up from below the horizon separating the real from the unreal. All too soon, large patches of deep blue were revealed. The storm had fallen back. My impulse was to turn away and start for home, but with no warning the pink of the sky turned the whole vast expanse of ocean to pink.

The last verse of the Night Chant of the Navajos, the *Yei-bechai*, came to me:

> In beauty, I walk,
> With beauty before me, I walk,
> With beauty behind me, I walk,
> With beauty above me, I walk,
> With beauty all around me, I walk,
> With beauty within me, I walk,
> It is finished in beauty,
> It is finished in beauty,
> It is finished in beauty,
> It is finished in beauty.

Each moment made the preceding moment a lie, but I could no longer look into the sun, it had already left black moons in my eyes.

The little lizard, in order to find out what was going on in the world, would play the flute. And the coyote, in order to take it in, would cock his ear.

The Eye of the Flute: Chumash Traditional History and Ritual as told by Fernando Librado Kitsepawit to John P. Harrington

CHAPTER NINE

The White Coyote

Tom, one of the cowhands, had seen a white coyote in the San Augustine; he said he saw him three times. The horse breaker also claimed to have seen him, but in the Bulito. It had to be the albino.

My brother and I used to hear rumors of white deer on the ranch. We were forever out scanning the distances, peering into thickets, making games for ourselves; if I closed my eyes at certain places and for specific counted-out lengths of time I might, on opening them, see the white deer. Our covenant was that if we saw one, we would never complain about anything, ever again.

Oddities like these occupied our fantasies in the wild world. Once I hoped to find a pony so tiny I could hold it in the palm of my hand.

And now, at my age, some of it might materialize. Tom swore the coyote he saw was white as snow. Tom had been raised by the Indians and could have adopted some of their potential for fantasy; he was like my brother and I when we were young—like the Indians, by instinct and through awareness and solitude. Tom, for instance, could not look you in the eye, or if he could, he wouldn't. Like Indians, he seemed to find white men's eyes too penetrating.

Soon after I heard about the white coyote I rode with the men early in the morning. No one talked. Men are never talkative in the early morning, especially on the ranch; they seem bent on keeping to their own thoughts—to the business at hand, or what was left and lingering from their dream world.

Boston City Club
January 9, 1913
To Clinton and Jane Hollister

Dear Clint and Lady Jane:

I got back here from New York this evening, and the club steward handed me a great big flat parcel, marked as from you. Bringing it up to my room, I opened it and found, not only what I expected; not only love; but love illustrated: a *picture of you: one picture of you two. I was delighted. It was a twin photograph, and if I thought you were looking and thinking of me, it would be a triplet. But I'll not be so conceited as to imagine that, though I have seen you both look at me in that same way. I'll keep the picture and if I ever have a home again, I'll stick a pin in you and hang you up where I can keep an eye on you.*

It's cold out here. I saw by the papers that you had a hard, cold snap in So. California also, and it may be the same one. For weather like all good things and some bad people, moves from west to east. Civlization goes the other way, so that's an exception. But I'm not, and some day you two will be coming east. Maybe it will be in a winter season. . . . Eastern children have some fun we Western kids don't have. But then, we have some fun that they don't have. We have the best of it, but neither we or they know it, so nobody is the wiser, except grown-ups, who can't have as much as either Eastern or Western children. We're not wise enough. We work too much and play too little, just as you play too much and work too little. Don't you? I'm not sure. I'm only guessing. Ask your mother. She knows, maybe. I don't believe your father does. He works all the time. He likes to work, but he is working for you on the theory that you won't like to work. And you will, or you won't be happy.

As for that dam of ours, what if it did break? We had the fun of making it, and it had the fun of breaking. There's a canal with two or three dams or locks at Panama. It's bigger than ours and took longer to dig, and more workers, but it is just like ours, essentially. Ask about it; it's a fine thing and, having built one yourselves, you will understand all about it.

I must go to bed. I'll be out there in February or March. I may not get to Gaviota, but I'll be passing by once or twice. And I'll not throw you my hat this time, only a kiss.

Love to father and mother, and you.

Your loving uncle,

Lincoln Steffens

What little talk there was had to have a point; important things, like horses. Tom, for example, loved a certain small colt. He cared about him so much he was named "Little Tom," perhaps because Tom is also small; at times he seems to appear out of nowhere, his extra-small body slithering like a wild thing, his unusually bright blue eyes alight in his pale ugly face.

That day the subject, such as it was, ranged around the fact that our ranch-bred colts are superior to some "old things" they bought by the carload recently. Dan, the horse breaker, was an authority. Our stud, for instance, was too long in the back and yet he threw good colts. The long back was not passed along. Then there was Little Tom, who had a full sister, and she was crazy. She was not as little as Little Tom, but she had the dwarf genes in her dish face. She would lie down so long with her saddle on that she seemed dead. "She is crazy in the head, she is no good, she will have to go to the dogs," the horse breaker said, meaning she would have to be made into horse meat. Tom listened quietly and then interjected that his Little Tom was growing to a thousand pounds, perhaps a bit more. He was already about 975 and he was as good as his sister was not. Tom and the horse breaker were uneasy with each other. The horse breaker had named Little Tom "Bugs" and still called him that.

The men were on their way to the Bulito west fork to round up the Mexican cattle and drive them out of the back canyons for shipping at the end of the week. The black bulls also had to be brought out of the canyons. Where they were going would make it an all-day job, especially because of the bulls. The Texan called Rich described with a flourish in his Texas drawl how he was charged twice and how he hightailed it clear over a ridge before the black devil quit chasing him.

We parted ways where the left and right forks of the Bulito joined. The roan, not wanting to leave the others, was indignant. Up to then he had been eager, had nosed right up to the front of the four of us, showing off. A pleasure ride was beneath the dignity of a cow horse, and his ears, as we turned off, no longer pricked forward but lay back flat and sullen. I had to tell him with a sharp cut of the reins across his flanks that he couldn't get away with it.

It was overcast and cold in the Bulito as it had been all spring, but there were many birds. I never before saw so many; it was surprising. Why does one always associate birds with sunshine?

The oaks, because of all the soft, kind rain, had separated out as individuals. A recent burn was healing over and only here and there could one see scorched oak branches—a bluegreen predominated on the range. One small, fat woodpecker could be seen bobbing on an oak. He wasn't even slightly curious about us.

Such a happy canyon; yet so dark from the overcast sky. It was a symphony of small sounds—the whirring of wings, the intimate bird-talk, not their serious singing, which is, after all, a declaration of territorial rights. A male and female quail couple meandered nearby, house-hunting. Most of the nesting should be over; noises should be coming from young birds seeking free service from their tired parents. Yet it was not quite like that, it was more an atmosphere of exuberance and the promise of things to come. And one knows that in good years many birds are prone to nest twice. This had to be the second time around. Families in good times sometimes overlap. Quite recently I saw a red-faced linnet with a gray, fat squab of a young one trailing after him, yelling his head off for food. At the same time the old linnet was singing his heart out for a lady well entrenched in a nest in the vines.

The whole left fork was suffused in a cold mist, the long arm of the Bulito nestling there comfortably, seemingly content to be thus obscured. As Old Roan climbed slowly and burdensomely out of the right fork to its ridge, the huge land trough of the right and left forks stood out. (A geologist once said it was created by a giant fault and is part of the overall lay that accounts for the twenty or more miles of our east-west coastal section; nowhere else on the west coast is there so sharp a change of direction.)

The roan's ears suddenly pointed away from where the men were shouting as they drove the cattle out of the left fork. There had to be something unusual to catch his attention like that; and sure enough, even to my slow human perception a furry smudge was revealed in the grass. A coyote had been watching our progress up the jeep road. The roan, knowing the smell of coyotes—those predators tend to nose around herds of horses, looking for newborn colts—was showing some concerns. I remembered my father describing a pair of them bringing down a young colt. One of the pair relentlessly drove it out of the herd while the other slashed at its sides until its entrails fell out.

Old Roan, his ears pricked, walked briskly to the crest of the hill. He was definitely nervous. Soon he was frankly snorting. A second later, a big handsome coyote showed itself bounding through the wild oats that were high and thick and strong enough to force the animal, tall and strong as it was, to jump high into the air to clear them. The coyote circled wide around us. It was edged in black, with a black nose, darkish ears, and more dark markings on its luxurious full tail. But its fur was a rich tawny color and the black edging gave it depth. It looked more like a fox, an enormous fox. Its markings added to its noticeably efficient character. There was not an inch of it out of keeping with a will to survive. Tall, slim, and powerfully framed, it was a formidable inhabitant of this remote place. It gave me a glimpse into what the ranchlands had been like when predators were plentiful and essential to the wild economy. Its fitness was a kind of precision amounting to perfection. It made him god-like in the animal world—independent of man, totally free, wild and curious, *out there*.

I had encountered Tom's "white coyote."

He kept running in great leaps through the tall oats, glancing back at us with yellow, other-world eyes. He was the reality; we were the illusion. The coyote figures in Chumash mythology; he is the clown as well as their supreme being. Seeing this handsome creature took me back to the time when, as a teenage girl, I had shot one. The excitement, the excruciating buck fever as he was disappearing over the crest of the hill, the hunting instinct were all crowded into that one instant when I shot. My father helped me cut off the scalp containing its two ears to take to town to get my three-dollar bounty.

That was the first and last time I killed anything. The dimming, wild, unforgiving eyes of that animal still haunt me.

Now, in my old age, the bare glimpse of a coyote has become a privilege. City people who never know how potent the wild can be must invent fantasies to fulfill their sense of something beyond their reach, beyond their finite lives.

The coyote taken out of its setting would lose its magic, its meaning, which must be comprehended the instant one is allowed to see it.

We had caught coyotes in traps. The memory of their yellow eyes looking beyond us—not seeing us, as though we did not exist—remains with me. They were telling us with their last breath that they would go where we could never follow. The coyote, brutally caught by a paw, slashed and made gory by its own teeth in its desperate efforts to free itself, never utters a sound and never gives up. Whatever the horror, suffering pain beyond imagination, a coyote dies glowering hatred. The dark pupils of its yellow eyes widen with hate up to the moment when their lights go out. The coyote's ruthlessness toward its own victim, slaughtering it in a second, is nothing compared to the slow torture of man's trap or bullet wound.

I had often witnessed the coyote's powerful merciless jaws at work, and their deadly precision. The chittering ground squirrel, cleverly decoyed by a coyote from the safety of its hole, would be disposed of in a matter of seconds by coyotes working in pairs—clever clowns playing on the squirrel's innate curiosity. One coyote would wander nonchalantly past, within sight, its partner sneaking up from behind as the squirrel emerged; and in a flash of its powerful teeth silence the chittering. In that split second it clamped down with the sound of crunching bone.

Another time, years ago, close to where I was that day on horseback, I saw one demonstrate real courage. I saw my big German Shepherd dog suddenly race down the hillside. He was after a coyote that kept, strangely, just barely out of reach. In the middle of the long, wide arc the chase took, the coyote jumped neatly off the trail and left the big dog, in the force of his momentum, skidding and careening down the trail. Suddenly the coyote was back within a few feet of my horse, brazenly taunting us. It was an invitation to give chase, and the coyote seemed baffled when I didn't move. Suddenly a tiny fat coyote pup waddled out in front of me. Before I could make a move the dog grabbed it, biting through its soft stomach. It died in my arms.

Those strange, distant, cold yellow eyes of the coyote somehow lead you back through time. To you, who are only a speck on the horizon of the ages, they speak of aeons. The ancient trunk of a giant redwood has the same impact when you look into its topmost branches; its trunk, like the coyote's eyes, send you voyaging back to the beginning.

The coyote must be my totem animal. One short encounter like that with Tom's "white" coyote and these thoughts crowd around me. As a child I lay warm and protected, night after night, in a bed on the wind-swept porch of our home but my spine tingled as I shivered in delicious fear at the long, drawn-out caterwauling songs of the coyotes ringed around the house. Long, thin, high, almost staccato yaps from the far ridges were sometimes abruptly shut off by gusts of wind, or when the animals turned their backs. Just as often, their singing could have come from the edge of the brush on the hill next to the house. Our coyotes were in no special hurry, for this was their entertainment: they had come to tease our dogs. The eeriness of their staccato barks ending in long wails could be hair-raising. The dogs usually answered with exasperated, irritated yelps. The coyotes, perhaps only a pair of them, spent hours—one on each side of the canyon—taking turns taunting the dogs. By morning the dogs were worn out.

At times, in my childhood, encounters with these creatures would make the tears come, although admitting it would have been unthinkable; now I still felt the same mixture of dread and delight.

Strange, devil-like beings—the sneak thieves of the animal world—they were clever; they were beyond anything we could imagine. They could walk thin as a stick, or loom up big and substantial; but they were never out of control of a situation. It was big news if one of our dogs ran down a young coyote and shook the life out of it.

Just then a distant yapping came up on the wind. It was at the moment of these memories and thoughts, but for some reason the sounds no longer stirred me as they had. Had they released a hold of some kind? Was it because of writing these thoughts in my notebook?

Old Roan sighed pointedly and slobbered some green slime on my shoulder. Wild, prolonged barking and eerie cries from the two coyotes below brought his ears back into focus, and we resumed our ride home. They could have been hunting cries to distract their victim, or they had caught our scent on the wind. One could never tell about coyotes.

The coyote, like the wind, appeared when it pleased. You were lucky to see it at all and then only when it gave you permission. You never came on it unaware; or almost never.

Not long after, I told them at the board meeting: "We will liquidate." It was as though someone else had made the statement—it came out of my mouth without warning and several

at the meeting recoiled visibly—they thought I would never come to it. That night I slid into a deep and peaceful sleep for the whole night long. I was given proof that more of me than I had dreamed possible had settled an issue of attachment; that finally I had acquiesced, had done the only thing possible for us to do with respect to that land; and that at last I had released my claim for good in that beautiful, indifferent wilderness—or it had let go its claim on me.

To complete this episode I need to go ahead of my story and report that four years later, the day that ownership of all our lands passed out of our lives to another owner, a coyote with a white tail flowing gracefully behind him leisurely crossed the road in front of my car. I felt honored. But you can never tell about coyotes.

We need to witness our own limits transgressed, and some life pasturing freely on where we never wander.

Henry David Thoreau *Walden*

CHAPTER TEN

The Roan

As I PULLED MYSELF UP on Old Roan that day a spasm of anxiety shook me—it could have been a fear that I might not make it. His reaction to my uncertainty made him disconcertingly independent; when I struggled he had a habit of looking around at me. Sometimes he prodded me gently with his nose. Knowing how gentle he was, I was embarrassed by my clumsiness.

Like most of our ranch horses, he would often step out from under me as I mounted and helpfully half throw me over his back. Snubbing him tightly by the reins this time made him swivel his hind end out of my reach, and falling short of my elevated perch I was irked. He was such a big horse and I am so short that it was hard to reach the stirrup. Although unnerved by these antics, I had to joke with the men standing around so they would not have to express sympathy for my plight; some of them were only a bit younger than I and would have to ride on into their seventies and even eighties, and no one would be around to feel sorry for them.

Yet once on the road Old Roan behaved more like a colt than an old horse. Even though he was fat, and the sweat poured off him, he stepped out and away in his best cow-pony style; his strength always came through to me and with it familiar feelings of exhilaration enhanced by the pure, cold, early morning air. I felt glad to be alive. The strength and vigor emanating from his huge body and his fine old spirit made me feel as if I were a part of him. His power woke old reflexes that had been slumbering. Leaning forward on his

withers as he moved into his rocking-horse gait, I relished first his single-foot stride and then his frank, open gallop. I fell into line with the whole of him. The largest part of me as I leaned forward could have been head and shoulders for his massive torso.

Toward the end of the day, signs of *finis* suddenly became apparent in the old horse I was riding. I had not noticed before how hollow-eyed he had become; he had the gaunt look of old age. When he climbed steep places he had to lean a little against the inclines. His inner leg, at each stop, was bent for resting. He seemed at times barely held up by the other three. Several times I wondered if he might not fall against the bank. It was clear he had needed more rest than usual; yet he pawed the dirt impatiently at the gate on the way home in the Bulito Canyon. He was tired and old, and he was anxious to get back home.

Old Roan was one of the very few left from our original herd, which had descended from Bess—a golden, long-legged, sorrel thoroughbred mare. Later, thanks to the genes of Cowboy, a quarter-horse stallion, our horses acquired more substantial, short coupled bodies. But after our native-born herd had died off it was necessary to buy horses from inland ranches, which was a serious comedown. They could not, would not, and never did get used to the ocean, for instance. Travel on the beach was never a pleasure for me after that. Their endless tugging on the reins to escape water annoyed me. Those dumb "bought" horses made me realize the superiority of our native ones. In addition, our horses' knowledge of the terrain of our ranch made an inestimable difference.

Once I was driving at midnight over the ranch road with the superintendent and his wife. We overtook one of the vaqueros riding home—it was his last chance to be in time for Monday's appearance on the job. He was astride his broad white mare that was walking steadily, but briskly, down the middle of the road in the pitch dark. Without a flinch she ignored our headlights; she seemed intent on her task. Then we saw that her master was hopelessly drunk, and his horse, by

shifting her body from side to side as she walked, was keeping him from losing his balance and falling off. The vaquero was oblivious. He never knew we were there, nor that the superintendent had had to drive the car off the road and around him in order not to disturb the horse. The mare obviously had been in the caretaker role before.

Horses, heading for home under another circumstance, would have trotted in their anticipation; not this one. She was the symbol of pride: her head up, ears pricked, sensitively caring for her rider. At the gate she patiently waited. He, like a sleepwalker, slid off, reeling, and opened it. How incongruous it was that this horse was no longer in the role of an obedient mount; she was instead a helpful, concerned

friend to her owner who, with his head bobbing forward at every step, looked more and more like a corpse.

Even the superintendent told us afterwards that he was once in such a predicament (through no fault of his own, of course, he added self-consciously). His horse, by keeping him aloft with the same compensating swings of its body, had delivered him safely home.

My own Uncle Will, a rather wild character, had celebrated with special abandon one weekend in Santa Barbara and decided to drive his two-wheeled buggy home across a most unusual shortcut—the new Alegría viaduct constructed for the train trestle. He was on his way to the Santa Anita Canyon, ten miles into the ranch where the original adobe headquarters had been home to him and his brothers. The overpass was at skyscraper height. In the dawn, and being more than usually anxious to get home (his judgment, of course, at its lowest ebb) he made real what had only been a fantasy to local travellers; instead of driving his buggy the long way around into the Alegría canyon and out again, he headed straight for the trestle. A footboard with no protective railings lay down the middle of the structure that would be barely wide enough to accommodate the locomotive. The mare sniffed the board and carefully launched herself onto the plank, the cart wheels bouncing over the ties. That horse brought Uncle Will safely to the bluff opposite, more than a thousand feet away. Horses seem to know when they must be in charge.

These were not the first times on the ranch that horses showed more sense than humans.

In a much broader sense, my old roan had done as much for me.

Turn a thing inside out, and see what it is; and
what kind of thing it becomes when it has grown
old . . . Short-lived are both the praiser and the
praised, the rememberer and the remembered;
and this is but a corner of this part of the world;
and not even here do all agree, no, not anyone
with himself; and the whole world, too, is a point
in the universe.

Marcus Aurelius *Meditations*

CHAPTER ELEVEN

The Miracle Man

OLD ROAN DIED the day I arrived at the ranch after a trip to Europe. He dropped dead in his tracks on the beach, from heart failure. "I killed him," the horse breaker said, with more emotion than I'd thought possible for him. He probably did; he rode him too fast over the heavy white sand when he was green from pasture and too fat. The ranch people were saddened. They loved the horse quite as much as I did. His death, after the signs of his aging on our last trip together, showed clearer than ever that time was moving against us.

After the manicured green of Europe the ranch seemed outside my reflex system, dwarfed, even provincial. I found little to say beyond how much I missed the roan and that the range was so very dry. But, slowly and surely the pale bronze of the range stood out clear against the blue, blue sea. Where else was there such a sight? In the west the sun's path made brilliant an already glistening sea. Five hours past noon, the sun in its nakedness was advancing over the Bulito. The slight shift toward its winter arc over the water was barely perceptible.

Then I had a totally new kind of experience that spoke further to the ending of our era. Instead of striking out overland with the roan, I flew by helicopter the length of the coastal ranch. The machine careened crazily over the rough terrain because of conflicting up drafts. A pilot servicing the offshore oil platform had invited me up to see his bird's-eye view of where I had lived so much of my life, the canyons and ridges

I had been observing at such close range and describing in minute detail. We flew from Gaviota to Point Conception and back, stopping from time to time on the rounded tops of our coastal hills to give a close-up "eyeball" to important features, like our gasoline tank.

It was my first view of Point Conception from the sea. I could understand why Cabrillo had called it *La Galera*; it indeed looked like the galley prow of a Spanish ship. (Viscaino later called it *La Concepción*, because he passed by on December 8, the day of Immaculate Conception, in 1602.)

This sight of Conception revealed what had been a lifelong secret. The bare, uncompromising, hardened, defiant promontory—a consequence of nature's power—that had been seen from inland and on the map, was diminished in size from the helicopter and made mysterious by the bleaching mist and thin fog. I had to interpret its meaning in the few moments that we hovered over it. It had been a great mystery to me: in Chumash legends, it was the point of departure of dead souls into the next world, as they followed the sun to its death (and—if all went well—ultimate rebirth). It is called by many Indian tribes "The Western Gate." Why?

In my mind's eye it was a monster's snout, its snuffling nostrils two large caves hollowed out by the violent sea charging round it all year long and by the unchecked winds up to and beyond 90 knots. Pawing the water into white foam, this great animal, like an angry old bull throwing earth into dust up over his back, refused to be moved; its bold thrust would hold its own.

We flew out beyond and over Point Conception at high noon, between shifts on the oil platform. The pilot, who called himself The Miracle Man, told me about his morning passenger: the fellow who bought the Union platform and its company for a hundred million dollars. He had gone out to see what he'd got. It seemed that the pilot was glad to finally have an ordinary citizen with him.

Up the coast with Miracle Man, I was kept laughing. In his reassuring, jaunty way, he made me feel safe. The first

look at our 25,000-acre coastal ranch from the air forced me to try to take it in all at once—no birds, no monkey-faced owls, no mice, no tender, tiny sage flowers, no coyotes. Reflection was entirely inhibited by the whirring roar of the machine and the heights. In one sweep: a lifetime of experience. And in that sweep, canyon after canyon looked alike. The prehistoric giant oaks were hardly more than nubbins; as if they could fit in the palm of my hand; as if I could put them in my pocket.

But the sight of the great curving ridge ending in Conception was, as the pilot said, "the point of the whole trip." I could have ridden the ranch forever and never have seen what I did in one instant. That ranch had never really been ours. It belonged to a much bigger system than the Hollister family.

It's a despairing prospect. Here we are, practically speaking twenty-first-century mankind, filled to exuberance with our new understanding of kinship to all the family of life, and here we are, still nineteenth-century man, walking bootshod over the open face of nature, subjugating and civilizing it. And we cannot stop this controlling, unless we vanish under the hill ourselves. If there were such a thing as a world mind, it should crack over this.

Lewis Thomas, *The Lives of a Cell*

Afterword

June 27, 1986

Chevron authorities locked our gates yesterday.

Our appeal for a stay has not been decided by the judges in the California Supreme Court, yet Chevron has started operations. At least, they have brought their heavy equipment onto our property. They intend to lay huge pipes along the coastline—one for sour gas and one for oil.

Their detectives are already stationed at each end of the ranch. Their new uniforms and helmets are spanking and up to date compared to our general dishevelment from the dust, patched roads and mended fences. The legal fees we have had to pay have made it impossible to allow us more than a minimum standard of maintenance on the ranch.

The story of how they have managed to do this is a human, or merely political one, but it happened some time after our original sale to an enterprising but environment-minded Los Angeles man who—sad to report—has since died. The property ownership went through the proverbial revolving door, becoming almost unrecognizable in the process. But that is another story, for another day.

Part of it involved parcelling prime wild land in the coast ranch in one-hundred-acre lots for individual owners, and my husband, Joe, and I bought one of them back.

Am I suspect as well, since one hundred acres now belong to me? I hope not; I am respectful of it in its wild state and consider myself its steward. Chevron claims it will restore the

land to its virginal state—but once raped, hardly twice a virgin. They could have laid the pipe at the bottom of the channel, disturbing only a narrow strip of underwater sea land. In that case, in an event of an explosion, the damage done to the wild coast, to the shifting, underwater life, and to those of us on land would be minimized.

But Chevron has chosen to tear into a fragile coastline. Their decision indicates that they feel this land is expendable and unimportant in the face of the public's need for oil, the army's insistence on preparedness, and an American need to go on being powerful—our "manifest destiny." I can only believe that their appearance on the ranch means just one thing: another expression of man's historical arrogance and hatred of nature. He cannot understand this vast land still unclut-

tered by civilization, so he condemns it. The land is unknow-
able: therefore, destructible.

A few of us deliberately chose to live as far away as possible from the playground beaches to find the sanity and health
the wilderness would give us. The others, living between us
and Chevron's pollution, are even more vulnerable. The one
or two families on the mesas bordering the ocean who hero-
ically refused to negotiate with Chevron, in spite of the huge
monetary settlements offered, will suffer the most.

Tepitates-February 28, 1987

The "right to take" was judged in favor of Chevron by the
Supreme Court in Sacramento. The pipeline for oil and its

partner, the one for sour gas, lying parallel to it, are in the ground. I am wondering how they can be adequately monitored for leaks.

They called me "sentimental" to cling to a financially losing proposition.

Ranching was always a struggle; but struggle fit the original character of this place. There were floods and droughts—and always the midsummer heat and January cold. Dust and relentless winds, drying out the land after too little rain, blow to hurricane proportions, driving the sand from the beach. Shipwrecks off Point Conception and Point Arguello and offshore winds that have driven fishermen's rowboats out to sea, and to their deaths, are witness.

But when millions of dollars are poured into the place, the struggle will be over. The winds will be controlled by special planting in the canyons and by cabañas on the beach. The droughts will be relieved by water wells or water recovered from the ocean. The dust will be laid under cement. Only fire can wreak some havoc and revive some need for wariness—a last reminder that man is not all-powerful.

June 29, 1987

There will be about fifty signs along the stretch. There will be mileage markers and indications of bends and turnings of pipe. These will be installed before the pipelines go into operation and will be read by fixed-wing aircraft once a week to observe possible problems. The wording on the signs is a miracle of economy and precision. It is the Night Chant of the White Man:

NATURAL GAS LINE

CAUTION

HIGH PRESSURE

POISONOUS

OIL

POISONOUS

WARNING

PETROLEUM

PIPELINE

Index to Quoted Material

126 Thoreau, Henry David. *Walden* as cited in *The Winged Life: The Poetic Voice of Henry Thoreau* Sierra Club Books 1966

134 Aurelius, Marcus. *Meditations* from *Meditations of Marcus Aurelius* Heritage Press 1956

138 Thomas, Lewis. *The Lives of a Cell* The Viking Press, Inc. 1974

Index to Photographs

University of California Press 1965
Photographs courtesy The Bancroft Library

Three thousand copies of this book were designed by
Mark Ong of Side by Side Studios, San Francisco.
Text type Sabon, on 80# acid-free Glatfelter.
Digital composition by Wilsted & Taylor, Oakland,
California. The first printing has been limited
to a hardcover edition.